Selections from
The American State Papers
Monograph Numbers 1, 2, 3, and 4

FRENCH AND BRITISH LAND GRANTS IN THE POST VINCENNES (INDIANA) DISTRICT 1750–1784

Clifford Neal Smith

CLEARFIELD

Monograph Numbers 1, 2, 3, and 4
Copyright © 1996 by Westland Publications
All Rights Reserved.

Monograph Numbers 1, 2, 3, and 4
Originally published
McNeal, Arizona, 1996

Reprinted, four parts in one volume, for
Clearfield Company, Inc. by
Genealogical Publishing Co., Inc.
Baltimore, Maryland
2004

International Standard Book Number: 0-8063-5240-X

Made in the United States of America

Selections from **The American State Papers**, No. 1

French and British Land Grants in the Post Vincennes (Indiana) District 1750-1784

Clifford Neal Smith

First printing, August 1996   rz

Reprint, November 1996   qz

FOREWORD

The American State Papers are official public documents printed privately long before the Congressional Printing Office existed. The printing of public documents during the very early Congresses was done without any general provision of law as to what should be printed. Even as early as 1829 the clerk of the House of Representatives reported that, for the period 1793-1803 not a vestige of manuscript and only a scattered few printed copies were extant. A contributing factor was the destruction of the Capitol building in 1814 by fire.

In 1821 a bill was passed which authorized the publication of 750 copies of all the documents that could be found. The documents were published by two private companies: Gales and Seaton, and Duff Green. Of the two publications, Gales and Seaton is the larger. The Duff Green collection of documents are less comprehensive than the Gales and Seaton collection, and there are many differences in the pagination, particularly in later volumes.

Both publishers appear to have divided the original documents into general subject categories: Foreign Affairs, Indian Affairs, Finance, Commerce and Navigation, Military Affairs, Naval Affairs, Post Office Department, Public Land, and Claim. For genealogical and family history researchers, the last two categories--Public Land and Claims--are the most valuable, and it is from these two categories that this monograph *Selections from **The American State Papers*** will be made. The Public Land category, in eight volumes, covers the period 1789-1837; the Claims category, in one volume, covers the period 1790-1823.

In 1972 an attempt was made to index all names in the Public Land and Claims categories of the American State Papers; the index, although monumental, is, however, not complete. All researchers are urged to read pages i through xxvii of

Phillip McMullin, editor, *Grassroots of America: A Computerized Index to the American State Papers: Land Grants and Claims (1789-1837) with Other Aids to Research* (Salt Lake City, Utah: Gendex Corporation, 1972).

The present *Selections from the American State Papers* are the selections, by narrower subject matter, from the Gales and Seaton edition, made by this compiler for the use of genealogists and family historians because the original volumes are now very rare and, no doubt, inaccessible to most researchers.

INTRODUCTION

Vincennes, County of Knox, July 24, 1790

Sir:

The absence of the Governor having made it my duty to carry into effect, as far as possible, the resolution of Congress of the 29th of August, 1788, respecting the inhabitants of Post Vincennes, I beg leave to report not only my proceedings under that resolution, but some circumstances which, in my opinion, ought at this time to be communicated, as very materially concerning the interests of the United States as well as individual settlers.

The claims and pretensions of the people have very generally been exhibited; but, notwithstanding they were early advertised upon this business, by proclamation of Governor St. Clair, given at Kaskaskias, in March Last, and have since been repeatedly called upon by me, yet I have no doubt there are a few instances of inattention and neglect, which I have provided for by publication No. 8, a copy of which is hereunto annexed.

For all the possessions which appear to have been made by French or British concessions, I have issued warrants of survey, as by the last page of Nos. 2,3,4,5,6, and 7, of the land records for the county of Knox, copies of all which accompany this report.

I have also directed that the four hundred acre lots to be given to every head of a family, should be laid off for the persons mentioned named in Nos. 1 and 2, and allotted, excepting those that might fall to the absentees mentioned in the pages b and c of No. 2, which are to be retained, as there set forth, until the pleasure of Government is known.

I beg leave, sir, to observe that there are a few instances where the ancient inhabitants (by removing from Vincennes to the Illinois country, or from that country to this place) cannot be included under the description of persons entitled to donation lands, and they humbly solicit that Congress would be graciously pleased to consider their situation, and permit them to participate in the general bounty.

I think it necessary here to remark, sir, that, although the lands and lots which have been ordered to be surveyed appear, from very good oral testimony, to belong to those persons under whose names they are respectively entered either by original grants to them made, purchase, or inheritance, yet there is scarcely one case in twenty where the title is complete, owing to the desultory manner in which public business has been transacted and some other unfortunately causes.

The original concessions by the British and French commandants were generally made upon a small scrap of paper, which it has been customary to lodge in the notary's office, who has seldom kept any book of record, but committed the most inportant land concerns to loose sheets, which, in the process of time, have come into the possession of persons that have fraudulently destroyed them, or, unacquainted with their consequences, innocently lost or trifled them away; for, by the French usage, they are considered as family inheritance, and often descend to women and children. In one instance, and during the goverment of **Mr. St. Ange** here, a royal notary ran off with all the public papers in his possession, as by a certificate produced to me: and I am very sorry further to observe that, in the office of Mr. **Le Grand**, which continued from the year 1777 to 1788, and where should have been the vouchers for important land transactions, the records have been so falsified, and is such gross fraud and forgery, as to invalidate all evidence and information which I might otherwise have acquired from his papers.

In addition, sir, to the ancient ossessions of the people of Vincennes, under French and British concessions here, is about one hundred and fifty acres of land, constituting a part of the village, and extending a mile up the Wabash river, in front of their improved claims, which was granted by Mr. **St. Ange** to some of the Piankeshaw Indians, allotted into small divisions for their wigwams, and by them occupied and improved, until the year 1786, when the last of them moved off, selling, individually, as they took themselves away, their several parts and proportions. The inhabitants now hold this land, parcelled out amongst them in small lots, some of which are highly improved, and have been built upon before and since 1783. But imagining that a confirmation of any Indian purchase whatever might virtually involve some future questions of magnitude in this territory, I have postponed all order upon the subject until the pleasure of Congress can be known; in the mean time giving the claimants my private opinion that they would be permitted to retain the, either by free gift or for some small consideration.

A court of civil and criminal jurisdiction, establed at this place by **J. Todd**, Esq., under the authority of Virginia, in June, 1779, and who eked out their existence to the summer of 1787, have during that long period, continued to make large grants of land, even by their own acknowledgements, and without more authority for so doing than is set forth in No. 9. Many of the concessions which have been exhibited to me, in their name, they deny to have had any knowledge of; and, indeed, there are some reasons to conclude they may have been forged in the office of Mr. **Le Grand**, beforementioned, who was a servant of the court, and in whose hand writing the deeds have all been made out.

I cannot find, from any information I have been able to acquire, that Mr. **Todd** ever delegated any power of granting land in this country, or, in fact, that he was endowed with it himself. On the contrary, I find by the acts of Virginia of 1779, that lands northwest of the river Ohio were expressly excepted from location, and that it was declared no person should be allowed pre-emption, or any benefit whatsever, from settling this side the said river; and the Governor was desired to issue his proclamation requiring all persons to remove themselves, and, in case of disobedience, to make use of an armed force. This is not to extend to French and other old inhabitants actually settled on or before that time in the villages of Post Vincennes and upon the Mississippi. It appears, however, by a proclamation of Mr. **Todd**'s, No. 10, given at Kaskaskias, the 15th day of June, 1779, that a kind of authority was meant to be implied somewhere in the country, to grant lands, not only upon the river bottoms and prairies under the French restrictions, but in large quantities, and with more latitude at a distance therefrom; and twenty-six thousand acres have been granted away from that time to 1783, inclusive; and to the year 1787 (when General **Harmar** checked the abuse) twenty-two thousand more, though generally in parcels of four hundred acres, though some are much smaller, and do not exceed the size of house lots. The court has also granted to individuals, in some instances, tracts of many leagues square; but a sense of the impropriety of such measures has prevented the bringing forward those claims. Notwithstanding that some of the four hundred acres and small lots, on or before 1783, yet the authority whence they were derived has been such that I could not consider them as "rightful claims." They are, however, sir, in a few instances, under considerable cultivation and improvement and some of the plantations and many of the small lots which have been granted by the court since that time, are now cultivated in tillage and have been possessed by the present claimants, at much expense; but by far the greatest number of them were obtained at the cost of office fees only, and remain to this hour in a state of nature, or with no other alteration than has been necessary.

Upon the subject of these lands, sir, a petition has been presented to me by, and on behalf of, eighty Americans setting forth that they were induced to come into this country by the court of Post Vincennes, with every assurance of their authority to make grants. That, in good faith of this, they have formed their establishments at considerable expense, and must be involved in ruin, unless the generosity of Congress shall permit their holding them.

The French inhabitants have also petitioned me upon the subject of court grants; some of which are now under cultivation, at no small expense and labor.

I beg leave, sir, to lay the sitution of those people before Government, most respectfully representing that the welfare and prosperity of a number of industrious and good citizens in this territory must depend very much upon their order.

A petition has also been presented by the inhabitants of Vincennes, praying a confirmation of their commons, comprehending about two thousand four hundred acres of good, and three thousand acres of sunken lands. They have been, it appears, thirty years under a fence, which is intended to confine their cattle within its boundaries and keep them out of their wheat fields; for, contrary to the usage of farmers generally, the cattle are enclosed, and the cultivated lands are left at large, except those parts which immediately approach the commons. But this fence, and quiet possion under the French and British Governments, they seem to imagine entitles them to a good prescriptive right. It has been the usage of the commandants to make all their grants in writing and, as this has not been produced, or any evidence of it, I think it my duty to refer the matter to Cngress, as I am not authorized to decide upon it.

One other petition, sir, I am constrained to introduce. It has been signed by one hundred and thirty-one Canadian, French, and American inhabitants, all enrolled in the militia, setting forth that many of them were head of families soon after the year 1783. That, from their situation, they are liable to, and willing to perform, an extraordinary proportion of military duty, and soliciting that Congress would be pleased to make them a donation of lands. In justice to the petitioners, I think it incumbent on me to observe that the commanding officer of the regular troops here has been obliged in some instances to demand their services for convoys of provisions up the Wabash river; and, from the weakness of the garrison, and the present difficulties of communications with other posts and the Ohio, that he may have frequent occasion for their aid, which I have no doubt will be yielded at all times with the greatest cheerfulness.

Before I close this letter, sir, I must take the liberty of representing to Congress, by desire of the citizens of this country, and as a matter which I humbly conceive they should be informed of, that there are, not only at this place, but in the several villages upon the Mississippi, considerable claims for supplies furnished the troops of Virginia before and since 1783, which no person yet has been authorized to attend to, and which is very injurious to the interests and feelings of men who seem to have been exposed to a variety of distresses and impositions by characters pretending to have acted under the orders of the Government.

The people of Vincennes hve requested me to make known their sentiments of fidelity and attachment to the sovereignty of the United States, and the satisfaction they feel in being received into their protection which I beg to communicate in their own words, by the copy of an address presented me on the 23rd instant.

If, in this long letter of report and representation, I may appear to have tediously dwelt upon the claims and pretentions of the peope of this country, I request, sir, that it may be attributed to that desire which I feel at all times faithfully to execute the attentions necessary to individual interests, and the great duty I owe the Government.

With every sentiment of respect to your Excellency and Congress, I have the honor to be, sir, your most obedient and humble servant.

Winthrop Sargent

ENCLOSURE NUMBER 1
(ASP 8:1:11)

Town at Post Vincennes, July 13, 1790

From the best information I have been able to acquire, confirmed by the testimony of the gentlemen of the Courts of Quarter Sessions of the Pace and Common Please, as well as Judge and Probate, given me in the presence of yourself, Major **Hamtramck**, and Major **Vigo**, I believe the following to be an accurate list of the heads of families settled at Post Vincennes, on and before the year 1783, and residents here at this time: Consequently they are entitled to the donation lands promised them by Congress; and you will please to consider this as your sufficient warrant for surveying and allotting them agreeably to the commission give you for that purpose. Patents will issue as soon as your returns are made into my office.

Winthrop Sargent

To **Samuel Baird**, Esq.

Joseph Andrez	Honorez Darrys	Andrez Monplesir
Louis Alare	Charles Dudevoir	Louis Meteyer
Francois Brouillet	Amable Delisle	Francois Minie
Vital Boucher	Jacque Denye	John Babtiste Milliet
Francois Baroye, Jr.	Joseph Ducharme	Nicholas Mayot
Marie, widow of Louis Boyer	Bonnaventure Derogier	Francois Mallet
John Babtiste Binette	Nicholas Ditard	Joseph Mitchel
Amable Boslon	Francois Desause	Antoine Marier
Charles Bonneau	Louis Edeline	Frederick Mahl
Charles Bugand	Joseph Flamelin	Joseph Malette
Michael Bordeleau	John Babtiste Joyale	John Babtiste Mois
Nicholas Baillarjon	Paul Gamelin	Michael Neau
Michael Brouillet	Charles Guielle	John Babtiste Ouilette
Francois Bosseron	Toussaint Goder	Joseph Perodeau
Francois Baroye, Sr.	Antoine Gamelin	Guillaume Payes
Antoine Bordeleau, Sr.	Pierre Gamelin	Pierre Perret
Louis Brouillet	Amable Gaurguipis	Amable Perron
Louis Boyer, Jr.	Alexis Asttase Gallionois	Pierre Quenez, Sr.
John Babtiste Cardinal		John Babtise St.-Marie Racine
Francois Coder	Pierre Gilbert	Pierre Regnez
Pierre Carnieyer	John Babtiste Harpin	Francois Racine
Joeph Chabot		

Antoine Cary
Francois Compagnot
Jacques Cardinal

Joseph Chartier
John Charpentier
Louis Coder
Jacob Charbonneau

Pierre Chartier, Sr.
Moses Carter
Antoine Drouettee
John Babtiste Dubois
John Babtiste Ducheme
Charles Dielle
Charles Delisle

Pierre Daigneau
Antoine Darrys
Louis De Claureier*

John Babtiste De Elaureier*

Joseph Hunot, Sr.
Etienne Jacques
Edward Johnston
Jacques Latrimouille
Francois Lognon
Joseph Lognon
Jacque Lacroix
Pierre Laforest

Antony Luneford
Charles Languedoc
Jacque Lamotte
Andrez Languedoc
Renez Langlois
Joseph Levrond
Louis Laderoute

Francois Languedoc
Louise Lamare
John Babtiste Maugen
Pierre Malette
Antoine Malette

Pierre et Andrez Racine
Louis Ravalet
Louis Roupiault

Joseph Raux
Joseph St. Marie
Joseph Sabolle
John Baptiste St. Aubin

Etienne St. Marie
Francois Turpin
Francois Trudel
Joseph Tongas
Francois Vachette
John Babtiste Vaudrye
John Babtiste Vaudrye, Jr.

Francis Vigo
Alexander Vallez
Antoine Vaudrye

John Babtiste Vilray
Nicholaus Charpaid

Angelic, widow of Etienne Phillibert
Mary Louis, widow of Nicholas Perrot
Felicite, widow of Francois Peltier
Louisa, widow of Andre Peltier

Angelic, widow of Francis Basinet
Marie, widow of Nicolaus Cardinal
Susanna, widow of Pierre Coder

Marian, widow of Louis Denorgon
Veronique, widow of Gilliome* Daperon
Francoise, widow of Ambroise Dagenet
Genevieve, widow of Pierre Gumare

Ann, widow of Moses Henry

Catarine, widow of John Babtiste Lafontaine
Maudeline, widow of St. Jean Lagarde
Veronic, widow of Gabriel Legrand
Marie Louise, widow of John Phillip Marie Legrats
Louisa, widow of Antoine Lefevre
Catarine, widow of Amable Lardoise
Maudeline, widow of Joseph Stone
Genevieve, wife of Joseph Labuissiere, the husband deserted
Renez Godere dit Pannah
Agate, widow of Amable Dumay
[* So spelled.]

[ATTACHMENT NUMBER 1]
(ASP 8:1:12)

The following list of names is certainly within the letter of the resolution of Congress; and it appears to me that they are entitled to donation lands; but the consideration annexed to the grants in the Illinois country, leave some doubts in my mind as to the propriety of decision until I can refer the matter. You will, however, lay off the necessary number of lots, to be for their use and benefit if Congress shall so direct, or otherwise to revert to the United States.

[To **Samuel Baird**]   **Winthrop Sargent**

Thomas Dalton. He was a military officer here on and before the year 1783, head of a family, and owner of lands, which he has not disposed of, but in the last year he went to New Orleans, where he is a tavern keeper.

William Hamilton. A settler and head of a family in 1783, but now resident in Kentucky; he has lands here.

Joseph Rouse. Head of a family here in 1783, sold his property and removed to the Illinois, but claims his donation lands at this place.

Andre Roy. Head of a family in 1783, now living at the Illinois, owner of lands, and also claims his donation lot Post Vincennes.

Louis Bergeron. Head of a family in 1783, has sold his property, and removed to the Illinois, but claims the donation lot here.

John Babtiste Chartier. Head of a family in 1783, has sold his property, and gone over to the Spanish settlements, but claims his donation lands.

Joseph Dube`. Head of a family in 1783, now gone to the Spanish settlements, has lands here, and claims the donation lot.

Guilbaut Charles. A claimant as **Dube`**, and in similar situation.

The widow of **Pier Peron.** Is gone to New Orleans, but left children at this place; her husband was the head of a family, and the donation land is claimed for the children.

N.B.: It is observed of these people that the scarcity of provisions and their poverty forced them away, but they will return.

Louis Lem..y. Now living at Kahokia.
Andrez Roy. Retains his property here, but is absent.
Francois Roussiant. Now living at Kahokia.
Ambrose Dumais. Has property here, but is absent.
Dennis Le Barge. Ancient settler, but absent.
Francois St. Marie. Ancient settler, but absent.

[ATTACHMENT NUMBER 2]
(ASP 8:1:12-15)

Sir:

You are also to survey, lay off, and bound, the several tracts and parcels of land hereafter specified, for, and at the expense of the proper claimants, and return plats thereof, as soon as may be, into the office of the Secretary of the Territory. And you will please to observe that the measurements of all ancient rights must be by the French acre or arpent, which has heretofore been the standard of land measure in this as well as in the Illinois country.

To: **Samuel Baird**, Esq.   **Winthrop Sargent**

For **Frederic Berger**. A lot in Post Vincennes, of twenty-five toises, one side to the church lands, another to **Andrez Montplesir**, and two others to streets.

John St. Aubin. A piece of land, two acres in front, and the usual depth, one side to **Nicholas Chasseau**, and another side to -- **Dayneaux**. A lot of one hundred and fifty feet, one side to -- **Levron**, and the three others to streets. Another lot, fifty-one feet by thirty, fifty-one feet by thirty; one side to -- **Regis**, another to the common, and two sides to streets. Another seventy-two feet by one hundred and fifty; one side to -- **Brisard**, another to unlocated lands, and two sides to streets.

To widow -- **Denorgon**. A piece of land three acres in front, and usual depth; one side to -- **Barr**, and the other to **Lappamboise**.

Michael Neau. A lot one hundred and fifty feet, one side to **Peter Coder** and another to **Louis Mallet**.

Charles Bonneau. A lot of one hundred and seventy four by one hundred and fourteen feet, one side to **Bene Coder**, one to **Charles Bonneau**, one to -- **Landeroule** and -- **Lafleur**, and one to main street.

Francis Mallet. A piece of land, two acres in front and usual depth, by the meadow of the Big Marsh. A lot one hundred and fifty by one hundred and twenty situated above the fort.

Nicholas Chapart. A lot two hundred and four by one hundred and eighty feet: one side to a street running to the water, another side to a street running to lands not granted.

Louis Edeline. A piece of land two acres in front, and customary depth, one side to -- **Dainaux**, another to -- **Sanschagrin**, and by the Big Marsh Meadow. One lot of twenty-five toises, one side to -- **Chabot**, and three sides to streets. A piece of land, four acres in front by the usual depth, one side to **J. L. Denorgon**, and other side church land.

John Babtiste Ducheme. A lot one hundred and twenty feet, facing three streets.

Michael Bordeleau. A piece of land, two acres front by the usual depth, one side to -- **Proux** and the other to -- **Buelle**. A lot one hundred and fifty by one hundred and thirty-eight feet, facing four streets. Another lot in the town on which stood a barn. The quantity and boundaries are not expressed in the original concession, and it must be laid off as not to interfere with the streets of the village, or lot of any other person.

Laurent Bazadonne. A lot thirty-eight feet wide, from a street to a lane--one side to **Louis Boyer**.

John Binet. A lot one hundred and fifty by thirty-two feet, one side to -- **Arpin**, another to **Charles Lachin**, and two sides to streets.

Antony Caty. A piece of land, two acres front by the usual depth, one side to **Louis Edeline** and the other to **Joseph Leveron**, near the Big Marsh.

Alexander Vallee. A lot one hundred and fifty feet, one side to **Francois Barois**, another to **Michael Neall**, and two sides to streets. Two acres, by the usual depth, one side to **Touissant Noyon**, and the other by --? **St. Louis***. [*possibly a street]

Joseph Tougas. A lot one hundred and fifty feet, one side to -- **Sansosy** and another to -- **Anoyon**. Two arpents in front by usual depth, by the marsh of Cathilinettes* one side to -- **Tougas** and the other **Louis Bergeron**. Three acres in front by usual depth, in Cathilinette*, a side to **Francois Barois** and another to **Joseph Raux**. [So spelled; elsewhere called a prairie.]

James Cardinal. A piece of land three acres in front and usual depth, on the other side the Hog Swamp, and joining the lands of -- **Lachine**. A lot twenty-five toises, one side to -- **Languedoc** and another to -- **Carron**.

Peter Mallet. A lot twenty-five toises, one side to **Lewis Mallet**, and the other three sides to streets.

John Toulon. A lot one hundred and fifty feet square, one side to -- **Bakus [Bachus?]**, another to **Jacques Lamotte**.

Nicholas Ballaidron. Two acres in front and the usual depth in the prairie of the Grand Marsh, one side to **Peter Godere**, the other to -- **Vaudrye**.

Nicholas Ballaidron. A lot three hundred feet by one hundred fifty, one side to church, another to -- **Moreau**. A lot one hundred and fifty feet, one side to -- **St. Jean*** and to two streets, other boundary not mentioned. [*It is not clear whether this is a surname or a place name.]

John Decker. A lot one hundred and fifty by one hundred fourteen feet in the common.

Francois Languedoc. A lot eighteen toises by twenty-five, one side to a street and one side to -- **Redyente**. A piece of land two acres in front by forty in depth, one side to -- **Plifford** and another to vacant lands.

John Babtiste Millet. A lot in the village, one side to **Peter Pecon** and another to **Francis Dagneau**.

Stephen St. Marie. A lot of twenty-five toises, one side to -- **Cardinal**, and another to -- **Raperault** and facing two streets.

James Walls. A lot fifty by twenty-five toises, one side to -- **Andres** and three sides to the streets.

Nicholas Myot. A lot twenty-six toises, one side to **Peter Coder** and the other to streets.

Alexis Ouilette. A lot twenty-five toises by twelve and a half, one side to -- **Bolon** and another to -- **Derozier**.

Vital Boucher. A lot twenty-eight toise, one side to -- **Cardinal** and another to -- **Dubois**.

The widow of **Joseph Leveson**. A piece of land, two acres in front, but the usual depth; one side to -- **Sanschagrin** and another by -- **Chaboute**, near the Big Swamp. Also a lot of twenty-five toises; one side by -- **Sanschagrin**, and the others by streets, both supposed to belong to **A. Languedoc**.

Andrew Languedoc. A piece of land, nine acres in front by the usual depth, to begin at the common fence towards the Little River.

John Baptiste Frichette. A lot of twenty-five toises, one side to -- **Hamilton**, and another to -- **Vigo**.

Charles Lacoste. A piece of land, two acres front to the usual depth; one side to -- **Lacoste**, and another to -- **Riendo**. A lot twenty-eight toises square, and house thereon.

The widow and children of **Nicholas Cardinal**. A lot twenty-six toises square; one side to widow -- **Tranbulle**, and another to **Peter Queret**. A lot in the village, twenty-five toises; one side to -- **Bonneau**, and another to the domain. A tract of land, two acres by forty; one side to -- **Berthuit**, and another to -- **Godere**.

Peter Queret. A lot in the village; one side to his father [-- **Queret?**], and another to **M. Vigo**.

The widow of **Antoine Lefevre**. A lot of eighteen toises, five feet by twenty-four toises, five feet; one side to -- **Bonneau**, and another to -- **Vaudrye**. A tract of two acres in front, and the usual depth in the Little Prairie; one side to -- **Racine**, and the other to -- **Crepeaux**.

Joseph Perredeau. A lot twenty-five toises; one side to -- **Trudel**, and another to -- **Bonneau**.

Joseph Perredeau the younger. A lot of twenty-five toises; one side to -- **Johnston**, and three sides to streets.

Andrez Monplesir. Two acres in front, and usual depth, near the Cathilinette [a prairie]; one side to -- **Lamotte**, fronting the river. A lot twenty-five toises by three streets, and a barn thereon granted by -- **St. Marie**. Also a lot twenty [blot] one side to -- **Bergen**, and fronting two streets reportedly belonging to -- **Brouillet**.

[blot] **Andrew Pelliere**. Two acres in front by the ordinary depth, by lands of -- **Diri**. A lot twenty- [blot] on side to -- **Astringus**, and another to **J. B. Richard [?]**.

The widow of **Charles Lefevre**. Two acres in front and the usual depth, in the prairie of Cathilinette, bounding on lands of -- **Dubras called the Italian**. A lot in the village, bounded by **M. Vigo** and three streets.

James Latrimouille. Two acres in front by the usual depth, at the Nut Point; one side to -- **Vaudrye**, and the other to -- **Goder**. A lot of twenty-four toises; one side to -- **Dagnet** and another to -- **Drouet**.

Charles Dudevoir. A lot of twenty-two feet by ten toises; one side to -- **Small**, and another to -- **Connoyer**. Two lots fifty by twenty-five toises, to -- **Binet** and three streets. Two acres in front, at the Nut Point, bounded by the ancient common fence and **Baptiste Ducheane**. Two acres in front by forty in length, at the Big Swamp Prairie; one side to -- **Mallet**, and another to -- **Bordeleau**.

For the church. Four arpents front upon the Wabash, by the usual depth. A lot where the church stands, about twenty toises for the church or Mr. **Antoine Gamelin**.

Louis Leneveu. A lot of twenty-five toises, one side to -- **Read**, and another to -- **Luntsford**.

Honore Darris [?]. A lot of twenty-five toises, on which is his house. Two acres of land in front by the usual depth, near the little river; one side to -- **St. Aubin**, and another to -- **Bourger**.

Francis Vachet. A lot of twelve toises square; one side to -- **Cardinal**, and another to -- **Dubois**. **Vachet** also claims, by purchase from the Indians, land in addition, sufficient to make the lot twenty-five toises; but I cannot warrant the survey of the latter part.

Francis Baril? Bard?. A lot of thirty toises; one side to churchyard, and another to **John Larue**.

The heirs of **Moses Henry**. A lot seventy feet by twenty-five toises; one side to -- **Bordeleau** and to three streets.

Rene Langlois. A lot twenty-five toises, one side to -- **Monplaisir**, and two others to **Charles Languedoc**. Two acres in front by the ordinary depth, at the Cathilinette [prairie]; one side to -- **Barois**, and another to -- **Bordeleau**.

Francis Vigo. The house where he now resides and two lots; one twenty-five toises square, bounding to -- **Queret**, and the other thirty toises by twenty-five; one side to -- **Latippe**. Also four lots joining each other, and twenty-five toises square each; on one of the lots is a house belonging formerly to -- **Saboulle**. Also, two acres in front by the ordinary depth, from the Elm Road, one side to -- **Connoyer**, and the other to **Michael Brouillet**; a continuation to the river is also mentioned in the claim, but this is an Indian purchase, and not now to be surveyed. Also, a lot twenty-five toises; one side to -- **Villenueve**, and the three others to streets. Also a lot twelve toises in front, from St. Louis's to St. Honore's street; one side to widow -- **Legras**. Also, two tracts of two acres each in front by forty deep, north side of the Wabash, and opposite the village; one side by a road leading to the prairies, and the other side by the lands of -- **Paquin**. Two lots twenty-five by fifty toises, and a barn thereon; one side to **J. B. Vaudrye the younger** and **Francois Barois**, and three sides to streets.

The widow -- **Astargus**. A lot one hundred and fifty feet; one side to -- **Laforet**, and another to -- **Boisverd**, and two sides to streets.

Philip Chats. A lot seventy-five by one hundred and fifty feet; one side to **Renez Langlois**, another to the widow -- **Peltier** and facing two streets. Another lot one hundred and fifty feet; one side to **Charles Berjon**, another to **Francis Basseron**, and to two streets.

Pierre Kerre, Senior. A lot one hundred and seventy-four by one hundred and fifty feet; one side to -- **Gaynolet**, another to -- **Harpin**, and two sides to streets.

Robert Johnson. Two house lots in town, on which his house now stands.

Late widow of **Joseph Brassard**. A lot of twelve toises fronting St. Louis street; one side to -- **Bassadon** and another to -- **Connoyer**.

John Baptiste Richard. A lot in the village; one side to -- **Boisverd** and another to to -- **Lafuellarde**.

Stephen St. Marie. A lot twenty-five toises, one side to -- **Cardinal**, and another to -- **Rapuault**.

John Baptiste Binet. Two acres in front on the river Wabash, and to -- **Dagneau** and -- **St. Pierre**, near Cathilinette [prairie].

John Dovritt. A lot twenty five toises by twenty-three, one side to -- **Delorier**, and three sides to streets. Also two acres in front by usual depth, in the Nut Prairie, one side to -- **Dennis** and another to -- **Connoyer**.

James Lamotte. Two acres in front by the ordinary depth, one side to -- **Joachim**, the other -- **Montplesir**.

The heirs of **Joseph Lafuillarde**. A lot twenty by twenty-five toises, one side to -- **Sucrot** and the other to -- **Richards**. Two acres in front by the usual depth, at the Cathilinettes [prairie], one side to -- **Godere**, another to -- **Barada**.

Francis Basseron. A lot twenty-five toises, one side to **Philip Chattes,** another to -- **Haslin**.

Francis Lognion. A lot twenty-five toises, one side to **Francis Brouillet** and another to -- **Corneau**.

Peter Laforest. A lot of twenty-four by twenty toises, one side to -- **Nicholas** and the other to -- **Caty**.

Louis Seguin. A lot eleven toises by twenty-five, one side to the widow -- **Gumau** and another to Mrs. -- **Hunot**.

Anthony Marie. A lot twenty-five toises, or nearly that, bounded by four streets. Also, a lot twenty-five toises, one side to -- **Marie**.

Allen Ramsay. A lot twenty-five toises, one side to -- **Cuntz** and another to -- **Bogle**.

Ursule Cointe. A lot thirty-six by twenty-five toises, one side to -- **Keepler*** and another to Church Lands. [*So spelled.]

Charles Bergaud. A lot twenty-five toises, one side to **Philip Chat,** another to vacant ground, and two sides to streets. Two acres in front, one side to -- **Vallez** and another to -- **Languedoc,** near the Big Swamp. Some of this land is sold to -- **Page,** and the boundaries are not well expressed. Care must be taken not to exceed the ancient possession.

Francis Campagnote. A lot of twenty-five toises, one side to -- **Meteiller**, another to -- **Brirard** and by two streets.

The widow of **Peter Grimare.** A house and lot, the boundaries not expressed, but to be surveyed agreeable to possession, not interfering with the streets.

Louis Coder. A lot of land twenty-five toises, one side to -- **Danis** and three others by streets. Two acres in front the usual depth in the prairie des Cathilinette, one side to -- **Laforest**.

Joseph St. Marie. A lot one side to **Joseph Andrews**, another to St. Louis street, and one side to the Wabash. Also a lot of twenty-five toises, one side to **Joseph Charretiere**, another to **John Baptiste Harpin**.

Louis Aller. A lot twenty-five toises, one side to -- **Villeray** and three sides to streets.

Amable Bolon. A lot twenty-five toises, one side to **Antoine Richarville**, and another to -- **Dubois**.

Joseph Hunot. A lot eighteen toises by twenty-five, one side to **Peter Peret** and another to -- **Laderoute**.

F. P. A. [Racine?] and **John Baptiste Racine**, heirs of **J. B. Racine**. A lot of thirty toises, from St. Honore street to the next ensuing street, one side by -- **Crely**. Two acres in front by the usual depth in the Little River Prairie, one side to -- **Brouillette** and the other to Madame -- **Chapau**.

Francis Boyer. A lot of twenty-five toises, one side to -- **Lafraniere** and the other to **Richard Francis Turpin**. A lot of twenty-five toises, one side to -- **Dagneau**, and the three others to streets.

James McNutty. A lot in the village, one side to Mr. -- **Boyer**, another to -- **Charbonneau**.

Joseph Chartier. A lot in the village, one side to -- **Small** and another to **Joseph St. Marie**. Two acres in front by forty deep at Nut Point, one side to -- **Charbonneau** and another to -- **Vaudrye**.

Michael Brouillet. A lot eighteen toises in front, one side to -- **Connoyer** and fronting St. Louis and St. Honore streets. Also a lot twenty-five toises, one side to -- **Charpentier** and two others by streets. Also a tract two acres in front, in Nut Prairie, one side to -- **St. Marie**, and another to -- **Codere**.

Louis Mallet. A lot twenty-five toises, one side to **Peter Mallet** and three others by streets. Two acres in front by the usual depth, in the Big Swamp Prairie, one side to -- **Nicholas** and the other to -- **Champagnotte**.

Antoine Bordelau. A lot of twenty-five toises, one side to -- **Dagneau**.

Antoine Marie. A lot twenty-five toises, one side by his own lot. Three acres in front by forty deep, in the Big Swamp Prairie, one side to -- **Page** and the other to -- **Hunot**.

John Baptiste Vaudry. A lot twenty-six toises and two feet by seventeen and a half toises, one side to -- **Gibault**, and another to Madame -- **Chapau**, and another to **Pierre Gamelin**. Also a lot twenty-five toises, one side to Mr. -- **Cartier** and to three streets. Also two acres by the usual depth, on the Big Swamp Prairie, one side to -- **Lafranieu** and the other to -- **Baillargon**. Also, two acres by the usual depth, in the Prairie on the Little River, one side to -- **Charretier** and the other to -- **Latrimouille**.

Francis Miny. A lot twelve and a half toises by twenty-five, one side to -- **Dubois** and another to -- **McNutty**.

John Baptiste Ouillette. Three acres in front, by the usual depth, on the mill creek at the Yellow Banks, where is a saw and a grist mill.

Thomas Dalton. A lot in St. Louis street, thirty-one and an half feet front, and extending to the river, one side to **Joseph Andre**.

The widow of **Louis Boyer**. A lot thirteen toises by twenty-five, one side to -- **McNutty** and to **Charbonneau**. Part of this lot supposed to be claimed by -- **McNutty**.

Jacob Pea. A lot of twenty-five toises, one side to -- **Wyant** and another to -- **Sullivan**.

Peter Bonneau. A lot of twenty-five toises, one side to **Antoine Lefevre** and another to **Peter Gamelin**. Also one acre in front by forty deep, on the Elm road, one side to **Honore Darris** and the other to **John Baptiste St. Aubin**.

Francis Dumais. A lot twenty-five toises, one side to -- **Bonneau** and another to -- **Lognon**.

Peter Connoyer. A lot where he now lives, one side to **Michael Brouillette**, and three sides by streets. Also, another lot nearly opposite, one side by the late widow -- **Brassard**, another to -- **Lachine** and in front by St. Louis street. Also, a lot sixteen toises in front, one side to **Michael Brouillette**, and another by a cross street that leads to the river and St. Honore street. Also, a lot fronting out on St. Louis street, and to the banks of the river, one side to Mr. -- **Vigo**, and another to widow -- **Legrand**. Also, a lot twenty-four toises, one side to -- **Delisle**, and another to Madame -- Cardinal and the two sides to the street. Also, a tract two acres in front, by the usual depth east of the village by the Elm road, one side to **Peter Querez**, and the other to Mr. -- **Vigo**. A small lot and house thereon, upon the bank of the river, formerly belonging to -- **Peltier**.

Antoine Vaudry. A lot twenty-five toises, one side to -- **Barois**.

Ursule Clermont. Two acres in front, by forty deep, in the Big Swamp Prairie, one side to **Peter Coder**, and another to -- **Lachine**.

Peter Perret. A lot twenty-five toises, one side to -- **Hunot**, and another to -- **Denoyon** and two streets.

Louis St. Aubin. A lot about twenty-five toises square, one side to -- **Toujas**, in rear of church lands, and by two streets.

Luke Decker. A lot twenty-five toises by fifty, one side to -- **Sullivan**, and three sides to streets. A tract of two acres in front, by forty in depth, on the river Du Chi, and one side to -- **Martin**. This tract is said to have been by a French concession but none has yet been produced. His house is built thereon.

Gennevieve Villeneuve. A lot of twenty-five toises, one side to -- **Ranger**, and another to Mr. -- **Bosseron**, and by two streets. Two acres in front, by forty deep, in the prairie of the big marsh, one side to **Charles Villeneuve**, and another to **Charles Bonneau**.

Charles Villeneuve. A lot nineteen toises by twenty-nine, one side to Mr. -- **Vigo** and on three sides by streets. Also, a lot to Madame -- **Cardinal**, -- **Delisle**'s lots, and **Pierre Bonneau**, and fronting two streets. Also, two acres in front by the usual depth, in the Big Swamp Prairie, one side to **Jean Lazarde** and -- **Chapart**, and the other -- **Hapelin**.

John Francis Hamtramck. A lot thirty-three by thirty-four feet, one side to another lot of his, and a side to **Adamhar*** **St. Martin**. Another lot bounding on the last, and one side Mr. -- **Bassadon**, in front to a street, and the rear to the river bank. [*So spelled]

Reverend Peter Gibault. A lot about fourteen toises, one side to Mr. -- **Millet**, another to Mr. -- **Vaudrye**, and two two streets.

James Charbonneau. A lot twenty-five toises, one side to -- **McNutty**, and on three sides by streets. Also, two acres in front by forty in depth in the Little Rive Prairie, one side to -- **Beloup**, and another to **Antoine Lefevre**.

Louis Ravelet. A lot of twenty-five toises, one side to -- **Metier**, and another to -- **Campagnote**, and by two streets.

John Baptiste Villeraye. A lot of twenty-five toises, one side to **Louis Allare** and three sides to streets.

William Page. A lot of twenty-five toises, one side to -- **Baillargon**, another side by next described lot, and two sides to streets. Another lot twenty-five toises, one side to last lot. A tract of land of two acres in front, which has been directed for survey under -- **Bengaud**'s name, and it seems is in dispute. Also a tract of land of three acres in front by forty in depth, in the Big Swamp Prairie, one side to -- **Marie**, and another to -- **Arpent**.

Nicholas Chapart. Two acres in front by forty in depth, in the Big Swamp Prairie, one side to -- **Villeneuve**, and the other to -- **Dagneau**. Another tract, two acres in front by forty in depth, in the Big Swamp Prairie, one side to -- **Mallet**, and another to -- **Roi**.

Vitalle Boucher. Two acres in front by forty in depth, in front by the Elm road, and one side to -- **Cardinal**, the other to -- **Ducherne**.

Ann Springer. A lot twenty-five toises, one side to **Andre Languedoc**, and three others to streets.

Peter Latour. A lot of twenty-five toises by nine, one side to -- **Turdelle**, another to -- **Bonneau**, and two sides to streets.

Touissaints Dubois. A lot of twenty-five toises, one side to **Peter Gamelin**, and another to **James Cardinal**, and two sides to streets. Two acres in front by forty in depth, one side to **Andrez Roi**, and another to **John Baptiste Roi**.

Charles Dielle. Two acres by front and forty deep on the north side of the Wabash, one side to **Paul Gamelin**, and another to **Peter Latour**. The original concession, or the best evidence of it, must be produced, before this survey is made.

Antoine Petit. A lot twenty-five toises, one side to **John Baptiste St. Aubin**, another to **Francis Languedoc**, and by two streets.

Susannah Bolon. A lot of twenty-five toises by twenty-four; one side to **Nicholas Mayot**, the other three to streets.

William Park. A lot of twenty-five toises, one side to -- **Cotis**, and another to -- **Guitar**, and two sides by streets. Two acres in front by forty in depth, in the Big Swamp Prairie, one side to -- **Richarville***, and another by **Peter Carter**. A lot of twenty-five toises, one side to -- **Ganuchon**, another to -- **Bawhus***, and by two streets. [*So spelled]

Robert Ficron. A lot of twenty-five toises, one side by **Stephen St. Marie**, and another to the next lot. A lot twenty-five toises, one side to last lot, another to -- **Lafremiere**, and by two streets. Those lots are supposed to be old French concessions.

Widow of **Gabriel Legrand.** A lot about fourteen toises in front, one side to -- **Connoyer**, one side to the river, and two sides to streets.

Amable Guarguepie. A lot of twenty by twenty-five toises, one side to -- **Bosseron**, another to -- **Dubois**. Two acres in front by forty in depth, at the Nut Point, one side to -- **Cardinal** and another to -- **Latrimouille**.

-- **Watts**, -- **McNutty**, and -- **Simson**. Two acres in front by the ordinary depth in the Cathilinette Prairie, one side to -- **Reaux** and another to -- **Dielle**.

John Baptiste Harpin. A lot twenty-five toises, one side to -- **John Small**, another to **Joseph St. Marie**, and to two streets. A tract of land two acres in front by forty deep, one side to Mr. -- **Page** and another to **J. B. Vaudry**. Also one acre in front by forty deep in the grand Marais Prairie, one side to -- **Perodeau**, and another to -- **Neau**. Also a lot twenty-five toises, one side to -- **Dockac*** and another to -- **Peter**. [*So spelled]

Gerome Crely. A lot eight toises by nineteen, one side to -- **St Marie**'s heirs, another to **Francois Borois** and on two others by streets.

Joseph Duchram. One acre and three quarters in front by forty in depth, north side the Wabash, one side to **Paul Gamelin** and another to -- **Carron**.

Amable Delisle. A lot twelve and a half toises by twenty-five, one side to **Nicholas Baillargon**, and another to **Stephen Bowyer**, and the rear to **William Page**, front a street.

The widow of **Peter Coder**. A tract of land, two acres in front by forty in depth, in the Grand Marsh Prairie, one side to -- **Baillargon**, and another to -- **Chabot**.

Peter Gamelin. A lot of twenty-five toises, one side to **Joseph Hamelin**, another to **Toussaints Dubois**. and by two streets. Another lot of eighteen by twenty-five toises, one side to **J. B. Milliet**, another to -- **Bonneau**, near to -- **Vaudrey**. Also two acres in front by forty in depth in the Cathilinettes [Prairie], one side to -- **Barois** and another to -- **Peltier**.

John Small. A lot about fifty-two toises in front on St. Louis street, running back to the river bank, and on two sides streets. Also a lot twenty-five by eighteen toises, one side to -- **Arpent**, another to -- **Shiskey**, and on two sides streets.

Louis Brouillet. A lot of thirteen toises, fronting on St. Honore street and back to the beach, one side to **Antoine Mallet**, and the other by a street. There seems to be some additional claim to a small part of a lot adjoining, which must be inquired into upon the survey; by the papers handed in it is very unintelligible.

John Tougas. A lot of twelve toises in front on St. Honore street, one side to **J. M. Barois** and three sides to streets.

Paul Gamelin. A lot twelve and a half toises on St. Louis street, and extending back to the beach, one side to **Adamher*** **St. Martin**, and the other by Calvary street. Two acres in front by forty in depth, north side of Wabash. This in two tracts, one bounded by -- **Ducharm** and -- **Gueille**, and the other to -- **Detau** and -- **Connoyer**. [*So spelled]

The heirs of **Daniel Sullivan**. A lot twenty-five toises by thirty-eight, one side to -- **Chabot**, and another to church lands, and by two streets. Also a tract eight acres in front and sixty in depth, fronting on the Wabash, originally granted to -- **Chapart**; four acres are to be on each side the Little River, whereon is built a mill. Two acres in front by forty in depth in the Cathilinette Prairie, one side to **Dominique Bergand**, and the other to -- **Laforest**. Another tract, two acres in front, situated in the Cathilinette Prairie, behind the ancient lands, and extending back to Otter Pond, one side to -- **Ballargon**, and old French improvement.

John Martin. Two acres in front by forty in depth in the Cathilinette Prairie, one side to -- **Meteller**, and another to the lot of -- **Sims** on -- **McNutty** and -- **Watts**.

Benjamin Bawhus. A lot of thirty toises by twenty-five, one side to -- **Ganuchon**, and on the other by the next lot and by two streets. A lot thirty toises by twenty-five, one side to the above lot, another -- **Meldrum** and -- **Park**, and by two streets. A tract two acres in front situated on the Grand Prairie west of the village from the Wabash to the Cathilinette swamp, one side to **James Dony's** and the other to **Alexander Vallez**.

James McNutty. A lot, south to -- **Page**, west by church lands, and by two streets.

Adamher St. Martin. A lot upon the Wabash, front to St. Louis street, one side to **Nicholas Perrot** and the other to **Paul Gamelin**. He claims this as a mortgage.

James Johnson. A lot twenty-five toises, one side to **Joseph Lafleure**, and by three streets.

Alexander Fowler. A house lot in the village, one side to -- **Decker**, another to **Baptiste Commefaux**.

Louis Meteiller. A lot twenty-six toises by fifty, one side to **Joseph Levron**, another to -- **Brizard**, and two sides by streets.

Peter Cartier. A lot twenty-six toises by twenty-nine, one side to **Francis Mallet**, and on three others by streets. Another lot of twenty-five toises, one side to Mr. -- **Vigo** and three sides to streets. A tract of two acres in front by forty, in the prairie below the village, one side to park, and other to **John Baptiste Lafreniere**.

John Baptiste Tougas. A tract of land opposite to the village, two acres and a half front by the usual depth. This was originally granted to -- **Noveaux,** with the addition of another half acre, which has been transferred. Mr. -- **Tougas** claims at this time three acres, half an acre of which having been tranted by the court, cannot be confirmed by me at this time.

Antoine Gamelin. A lot of about thirty toises, fronting on St. Honore street and running to the Wabash. This lot, it appears from certificates, was originally granted to the church, and has been by the church wardens exchanged for the ground upon which the church now stands. It will be confirmed either by the church or Mr. -- **Gamelin.**

Vincennes, July 31, 1790.   **Winthrop Sargent**

Claims Rejected for Want of Evidence
(ASP 8:1:299)

Ancient French or British Grants

In whose right claimed	Present claimants	Quantity
-- Carrierre	Heirs of Carrierre	50
-- Carrierre	Heirs of Carrierre	68
Racine, Mary	Mary Racine	68
Ste. Marie, Pierre	Pierre Ste. Marie	50

Claims under Court Deeds

In whose right claimed	Present Claimants	Quantity
Ails, Amos	Amos Ails	400
Ails, Amos	Amos Ails	400
Ails, Stephen	Amos Ails	400
Ails, Stephen	Amos Ails	400
Brown, William	John Armstrong	423
Bergman, Christian	Alexander Fowler	340
Barrackman, John	John Barrackman	400
Bradley, Samuel	Samuel Bradley	400
Beckes, Permenas	Abraham Johnson	400
Brown, Joseph	Amos Ails	400
Brown, Frances	Frances Brown	400
Blackford, John	John Blackford	136
Blackford, Reuben	Heirs of Reuben Blackford	136
Brown, James	James Brown	136
Cooperwriter, Henry	Henry Cooperwriter	340
Cooperwriter, George	Heirs of George Cooperwriter	340
Cedeter, Jacob	Christian Howe	340
Cardine, John	William Cochran	340
Cardine, John	Alexander Fowler	34
Cardine, John	Alexander Fowler	136
Carmichael, Patrick	Patrick Carmichael	136
Devens, Samuel	Samuel Devens	400

In whose right claimed	Present Claimants	Quantity
Day, John	John Day	400
Day, Robert	Robert Day	400
Dixon, Henry	Amos Ails	340
Hamilton, William	William Hamilton	400
Howel, David	John R. Jones	340
Howel, William	John R. Jones	340
Henry, Moses	Daniel Sullivan, two tracts	340 & 200
Howel, Randre* [*So spelled]	Ralph Blackford	136
Jennings, Robert	Heirs of Robert Jennings	340
Lunsford, Anthony	Heirs of Anthony Lunsford	340
Legrand, Gabriel	John Armstrong	136
Long, Benjamin	Benjamin Long	340
Morrison, John	John Morrison	136
Morrison, William	Heirs of William Morrison	340
M'Clelland, John	John M'Clelland	340
Nangle, Andrew	Andrew Nangle	120
Pyat, Benjamin	Samuel Bradley	340
Philips, Henry	Amos Ails	400
Popenoe, Peter	Heirs of Peter Popenoe	340
Radley, John (Bradley)	Samuel Bradley	400
Robinson, Andrew	Andrew Robinson	400
Squires, David	David Squires	400
Sinnet, Richard	Richard Sinnet	136
Thomas, James	Amos Ails	340
Wyant, Christopher	Alexander Fowler	136
Wilson, Thomas	Thomas Wilson	400
Worthington, Wm.	Samuel Bradley	340
Worthington, James	James Worthington	400
Wyant, Jacob	Jacob Wyant	136
Wilkes, Joseph	Joseph Wilkes	340

Claims in right of improvements
(ASP 8:1:300)

In whose right claimed	Present Claimants	Quantity
Bordeleau, Michel	Michel Bordeleau	400
Bordeleau, Antoine	Heirs of Antoine Bordeleau	400
Barrois, Jean Baptiste	Jean Baptiste Barrois	400

Bradley, Charles	Charles Bradley	400
Bradley, James	Charles Bradley	400
Compagnotte, Pierre	Pierre Compagnotte	136
Danis, Honore	Heirs of Honore Danis	400
Edeline, Louis	Heirs of Louis Edeline	400
Fernsley, James	James Fernsley	400
Forney, Anthony	Stace M'Donough	400
Gamelin, Magdalene	Magdalene Gamelin	140
Grimarre, Pierre, Sen.	Heirs of Pierre Grimarre	102
Hill, Thomas	Stace M'Donough	400
Lunsford, Anthony	Heirs of Anthony Lunsford	400
Latrimouille, Jacques	Jacques Latrimouille	400
M'Mullin, James	James M'Mullin	400
Mallet, Pierre	Pierre Mallet	400
M'Queen, James	James M'Queen	400
Mays, Robert	Robert Mays	400
M'Queen, Benjamin	Benjamin M'Queen	400
Mills, Thomas	Thomas Mills	340
Pea, Henry	Henry Pea	400
Popenoe, Peter	Peter Popenoe	244 10p.
Ravalet, Louis	Louis Ravalet	68
Seguin, Louis (Laderoute)	Louis Seguin (Laderoute)	400
Ste. Marie, Joseph	Robert Buntin	136
Thompson, Joseph	Joseph Thompson	400
Wilson, Thomas	Thomas Wilson	400

Claims for the donations as heads of families
(ASP 8:1:300)

In whose right claimed	Present Claimants	Quantity
Bonneau, Nicholas	Nicholas Bonneau	400
Bailey, John	John Bailey	400
Bartheaume, Noel	Noel Bartheaume	400
Bolon, Hyppolite	Hyppolite Bolon	400
Billet, Pierre (Beausoleil)	Pierre Billet	400
Cornoyer, Louis	Louis Cornoyer	400
Chicot, Francois	Joseph Tougas	400
Johnson, Ezekiel	Ezekiel Johnson	400
Levron, -- widow	Widow -- Levron	400
Larche, Joseph	Larche, Joseph	400
Lecointe, Francois	Francois Lecointe	400

Morrison, John	John Morrison	400
Richard, Marie Josephe	Pierre Querre and wife	400
Rimbault, Pierre, Sen.	Pierre Rimbault	400
Racine, Andrew	Samuel Baird	400
Ravalet, Jean Baptiste	Louis Ravalet	400
Roderigo, Diego	Laurent Bazadon	400

Claim to the donation as militia men
(ASP 8:1:300)

Carson, Alexander	Alexander Carson	100
Davis, Cornelius	Cornelius Davis	100
Hinton, Vachel	Vachel Hinton	100
L'Esperance, Jean Baptiste	Jean Baptiste L'Esperance	100
Morrison, William	William Morrison	100
M'Mullen, James	James M'Mullen	100
M'Queen, James	James M'Queen	100
M'Queen, Benjamin	Benjamin M'Queen	100
Robison, James	James Robinson	100

Bonneau, --, 19
Bonneau, --, 20
Bonneau, --, 22
Bonneau, Charles, 06
Bonneau, Charles, 10
Bonneau, Charles, 10
Bonneau, Charles, 19
Bonneau, Nicholas, 27
Bonneau, Peter, 18
Bonneau, Pierre, 19
Bordelau, Antoine, 18
Bordeleau, --, 14
Bordeleau, --, 14
Bordeleau, --, 14
Bordeleau, Antoine, 26
Bordeleau, Antoine, heirs of, 26
Bordeleau, Antoine, Sr., 06
Bordeleau, Michael, 06
Bordeleau, Michael, 11
Bordeleau, Michel, 26
Borois, Francois, 22
Boslon, Amable, 06
Bosseron, --, 19
Bosseron, --, 21
Bosseron, Francois, 06
Boucher, Vital, 06
Boucher, Vitalle, 20
Bourger, --, 14
Bowyer, Stephen, 22
Boyer, --, 17
Boyer, Francis, 17
Boyer, Louis, 11
Boyer, Louis, Jr., 06
Boyer, Louis, widow of, 18
Boyer, Marie, widow of Louis Boyer, 06
Bradley, Charles, 27
Bradley, James, 27
Bradley, Samuel, 25
Bradley, Samuel, 26
Bradley, Samuel, 26
Bradley, Samuel, 26
Brassard, --, widow of, 19
Brassard, Joseph, widow of, 15
Brirard, --, 17
Brisard, --, 10
Brizard, --, 23
Brouillet, --, 13
Brouillet, Francis, 16
Brouillet, Francois, 06

Brouillet, Louis, 06
Brouillet, Louis, 22
Brouillet, Michael, 06
Brouillet, Michael, 15
Brouillet, Michael, 17
Brouillette, --, 17
Brouillette, Michael, 19
Brouillette, Michael, 19
Brown, Frances, 25
Brown, James, 25
Brown, Joseph, 25
Brown, William, 25
Buelle, --, 11
Bugand, Charles, 06
Buntin, Robert, 27
Campagnote, --, 20
Campagnote, Francis, 17
Cardinal, --, 12
Cardinal, --, 12
Cardinal, --, 14
Cardinal, --, 15
Cardinal, --, 20
Cardinal, --, 21
Cardinal, --, Mrs., 19
Cardinal, Jacques, 07
Cardinal, James, 11
Cardinal, James, 21
Cardinal, John Baptiste, 06
Cardinal, Marie, widow of Nicolaus Cardinal, 07
Cardinal, Nicholas, widow & children of, 13
Cardine, John, 25
Carmichael, Patrick, 25
Carnieyer, Pierre, 06
Carrierre, --, 25
Carrierre, --, heirs of, 25
Carron, --, 12
Carron, --, 22
Carson, Alexander, 28
Carter, Moses, 07
Carter, Peter, 21
Cartier, --, 18
Cartier, Peter, 23
Cary, Antoine, 07
Caty, --, 16
Caty, Antony, 11
Cedeter, Jacob, 25
Chabot, --, 11
Chabot, --, 22
Chabot, --, 23

Chabot, Joseph, 06
Chaboute, --, 12
Champagnotte, --, 18
Chapart, --, 20
Chapart, --, 23
Chapart, Nicholas, 11
Chapart, Nicholas, 20
Chapau, --, Mrs. 17
Chapau, --, Mrs. 18
Charbonneau, --, 17
Charbonneau, --, 17
Charbonneau, --, 18
Charbonneau, Jacob, 07
Charbonneau, James, 20
Charles, Guilbaut, 08
Charpaid, Nicholaus, 07
Charpentier, --, 17
Charpentier, John 07
Charretier, --, 18
Charretiere, Joseph, 17
Chartier, John Babtiste, 08
Chartier, Joseph, 07
Chartier, Joseph, 17
Chartier, Pierre, Sr., 07
Chasseau, Nicholas, 10
Chat, Philip, 16
Chats, Philip, 15
Chattes, Philip, 16
Chicot, Francois, 27
Clermont, Ursule, 19
Cochran, William, 25
Coder, Bene, 10
Coder, Francois, 06
Coder, Louis, 07
Coder, Louis, 17
Coder, Peter, 10
Coder, Peter, 12
Coder, Peter, 19
Coder, Peter, widow of, 22
Coder, Susanna, widow of Pierre Coder, 07
Codere, --, 18
Cointe, Ursule, 16
Commefaux, Baptiste, 23
Compagnot, Francois, 07
Compagnotte, Pierre, 27
Connoyer, --, 14
Connoyer, --, 15
Connoyer, --, 15
Connoyer, --, 16

Connoyer, --, 17
Connoyer, --, 21
Connoyer, --, 22
Connoyer, Peter, 19
Cooperwriter, George, 25
Cooperwriter, George, heirs of, 25
Cooperwriter, Henry, 25
Corneau, --, 16
Cornoyer, Louis, 27
Cotis, --, 21
Crely, --, 17
Crely, Gerome, 22
Crepeaux, --, 13
Cuntz, --, 16
Dagenet, Francoise, widow of Ambroise Dagenet, 07
Dagneau, --, 16
Dagneau, --, 17
Dagneau, --, 18
Dagneau, --, 20
Dagneau, Francis, 12
Dagnet, --, 14
Daigneau, Pierre, 07
Dainaux, --, 11
Dalton, Thomas, 08
Dalton, Thomas, 18
Danis, --, 17
Danis, Honore, 27
Danis, Honore, heirs of, 27
Daperon, Veronique, widow of Gilliome Daperon, 07
Darris, Honore, 14
Darris, Honore, 18
Darrys, Antoine, 07
Darrys, Honorez, 06
Davis, Cornelius, 28
Day, John, 26
Day, Robert, 26
Dayneaux, --, 10
De Claureier, Louis, 07
De Elaureier, John Babtiste, 07
Decker, --, 23
Decker, John, 12
Decker, Luke, 19
Delisle, --, 19
Delisle, --, 19
Delisle, Amable, 06
Delisle, Amable, 22
Delisle, Charles, 07
Delorier, --, 16
Dennis, --, 16

Denorgon, --, widow of, 10
Denorgon, J. L., 11
Denorgon, Marian, widow of Louis Denorgon, 07
Denoyon, --, 19
Denye, Jacque, 06
Derogier, Bonnaventure, 06
Derozier, --, 12
Desause, Francois, 06
Detau, --, 22
Devens, Samuel, 25
Dielle, --, 21
Dielle, Charles, 07
Dielle, Charles, 21
Diri, --, 13
Ditard, Nicholas, 06
Dixon, Henry, 26
Dockac, --, 22
Dony, James, 23
Dovritt, John, 16
Drouet, --, 14
Drouettee, Antoine, 07
Dube, Joseph, 08
Dube, Joseph, 08
Dubois, --, 12
Dubois, --, 14
Dubois, --, 17
Dubois, --, 18
Dubois, --, 21
Dubois, John Babtiste, 07
Dubois, Touissaints, 21
Dubois, Toussaints, 22
Dubras, --, called the Italian, 14
Ducharm, --, 22
Ducharme, Joseph, 06
Ducheme, John Babtiste, 07
Ducheme, John Babtiste, 11
Ducherne, --, 20
Duchese, Baptiste, 14
Duchram, Joseph, 22
Dudevoir, Charles, 06
Dudevoir, Charles, 14
Dumais, Ambrose, 09
Dumais, Francis, 19
Dumay, Agate, widow of Amable Dumay, 07
Edeline, Louis, 06
Edeline, Louis, 11
Edeline, Louis, 11
Edeline, Louis, 27
Edeline, Louis, heirs of, 27

Fernsley, James, 27
Ficron, Robert, 21
Flamelin, Joseph, 06
Forney, Anthony, 27
Fowler, Alexander, 23
Fowler, Alexander, 25
Fowler, Alexander, 25
Fowler, Alexander, 26
Frichette, John Baptiste, 13
Gallionois, Alexis Asttase, 06
Gamelin, Antoine, 06
Gamelin, Antoine, 14
Gamelin, Antoine, 24
Gamelin, Magdalene, 27
Gamelin, Paul, 06
Gamelin, Paul, 21
Gamelin, Paul, 22
Gamelin, Paul, 22
Gamelin, Paul, 23
Gamelin, Peter, 18
Gamelin, Peter, 21
Gamelin, Peter, 22
Gamelin, Pierre, 06
Gamelin, Pierre, 18
Ganuchon, --, 21
Ganuchon, --, 23
Gaurguipis, Amable, 06
Gaynolet, --, 15
Gibault, --, 18
Gibault, Peter, Reverend, 20
Gilbert, Pierre, 06
Goder, --, 14
Goder, Toussaint, 06
Godere, --, 13
Godere, --, 16
Godere, Peter, 12
Godere, Renez, dit Pannah, 07
Grimare, Peter, widow of, 17
Grimarre, Pierre, Senior, 27
Grimarre, Pierre, Senior, heirs of, 27
Guarguepie, Amable, 21
Gueille, --, 22
Guielle, Charles, 06
Guitar, --, 21
Gumare, Genevieve, widow of Pierre Gumare, 07
Gumau, --, 16
Hamelin, Joseph, 22
Hamilton, --, 13
Hamilton, William, 08

Hamilton, William, 26
Hamtramck, --, Major, 06
Hamtramck, John Francis, 20
Hapelin, --, 20
Harmar, --, General, 03
Harpin, --, 15
Harpin, John Babtiste, 06
Harpin, John Baptiste, 17
Harpin, John Baptiste, 21
Haslin, --, 16
Henry, Ann, widow of Moses Henry, 07
Henry, Moses, 14
Henry, Moses, 26
Hill, Thomas, 27
Hinton, Vachel, 28
Howe, Christian, 25
Howel, David, 26
Howel, Randre, 26
Howel, William, 26
Hunot, --, 18
Hunot, --, 19
Hunot, --, Mrs., 16
Hunot, Joseph, 17
Hunot, Joseph, Sr., 07
Jacques, Etienne, 07
Jennings, Robert, 26
Jennings, Robert, heirs of, 26
Joachim, --, 16
Johnson, Abraham, 25
Johnson, Ezekiel, 27
Johnson, James, 23
Johnson, Robert, 15
Johnston, --, 13
Johnston, Edward, 07
Jones, John R., 26
Joyale, John Babtiste, 06
Keepler, --, 16
Kepler. See Keepler
Kerre, Pierre, Senior, 15
Kuntz. See Cuntz
L'Esperance, Jean Baptiste, 28
Labuissiere, Genevieve, wife of Joseph Labuissiere, 07
Lachin, Charles, 11
Lachine, --, 12
Lachine, --, 19
Lachine, --, 19
Lacoste, --, 13
Lacoste, Charles, 13
Lacroix, Jacque, 07

Laderoute, --, 17
Laderoute, Louis, 07
Laderoute. See Seguin
Lafleur, --, 10
Lafleure, Joseph, 23
Lafontaine, Catarine, widow of John Babtiste Lafontaine, 07
Laforest, --, 17
Laforest, --, 23
Laforest, Peter, 16
Laforest, Pierre, 07
Laforet, --, 15
Lafraniere, --, 17
Lafranieu, --, 18
Lafremiere, --, 21
Lafreniere, John Baptiste, 23
Lafuellarde, --, 15
Lafuillarde, Joseph, 16
Lagarde, Maudeline, widow of St. Jean Lagarde, 07
Lamare, Louise, 07
Lamotte, --, 13
Lamotte, Jacque, 07
Lamotte, Jacques, 12
Lamotte, James, 16
Landeroule, --, 10
Langlois, Rene, 14
Langlois, Renez, 07
Langlois, Renez, 15
Languedoc, --, 12
Languedoc, --, 16
Languedoc, A., 13
Languedoc, Andre, 20
Languedoc, Andrew, 13
Languedoc, Andrez, 07
Languedoc, Charles, 07
Languedoc, Charles, 14
Languedoc, Francis, 21
Languedoc, Francois, 07
Languedoc, Francois, 12
Lappamboise, --, 10
Larche, Joseph, 27
Lardoise, Catarine, widow of Amable Lardoise, 07
Larue, John, 14
Latippe, --, 15
Latour, Peter, 20
Latour, Peter, 21
Latrimouille, --, 18
Latrimouille, --, 21
Latrimouille, Jacques, 07
Latrimouille, Jacques, 27

Latrimouille, James, 14
Lazarde, Jean, 20
LeBarge, Dennis, 09
Lecointe, Francois, 27
Lefevre, Antoine, 18
Lefevre, Antoine, 20
Lefevre, Antoine, widow of, 13
Lefevre, Charles, widow of. 14
Lefevre, Louisa, widow of Antoine Lefevre, 07
LeGrand, --, 02
LeGrand, --, 03
Legrand, --, 19
Legrand, Gabriel, 26
Legrand, Gabriel, widow of, 21
Legrand, Veronic, widow of Gabriel Legrand, 07
Legras, --, 15
Legrats, Marie Louise, widow of John Phillip Marie Legrats, 07
Lem..y.., Louis, 09
Leneveu, Louis, 14
Leveron, Joseph, 11
Leveson, Joseph, widow of, 12
Levron, --, 10
Levron, --, widow of, 27
Levron, Joseph, 23
Levrond, Joseph, 07
Lognion, Francis, 16
Lognon Joseph, 07
Lognon, --, 19
Lognon, Francois, 07
Long, Benjamin, 26
Luneford. See Lunsford
Lunsford, Anthony, 26
Lunsford, Anthony, 27
Lunsford, Anthony, heirs of, 26
Lunsford, Anthony, heirs of, 27
Lunsford, Antony, 07
Luntsford, --, 14
M'Clelland, John, 26
M'Donough, Stace, 27
M'Donough, Stace, 27
M'Mullen, James, 28
M'Mullin, James, 27
M'Queen, Benjamin, 27
M'Queen, Benjamin, 28
M'Queen, James, 27
M'Queen, James, 28
Mahl, Frederick, 06
Malette, Antoine, 07
Malette, Joseph, 06

Malette, Pierre, 07
Mallet, --, 14
Mallet, --, 20
Mallet, Antoine, 22
Mallet, Francis, 10
Mallet, Francis, 23
Mallet, Francois, 06
Mallet, Lewis, 12
Mallet, Louis, 10
Mallet, Louis, 18
Mallet, Peter, 12
Mallet, Peter, 18
Mallet, Pierre, 27
Marie, --, 16
Marie, --, 20
Marie, Anthony, 16
Marie, Antoine, 18
Marier, Antoine, 06
Martin, --, 19
Martin, John, 23
Maugen, John Babtiste, 07
Mayot, Nicholas, 06
Mayot, Nicholas, 21
Mays, Robert, 27
McClelland. See M'Clelland
McDonough. See M'Donough
McMullen. See M'Mullen
McMullin. See M'Mullin
McNutty, --, 18
McNutty, --, 18
McNutty, --, 20
McNutty, --, 21
McNutty, --, 23
McNutty, James, 17
McNutty, James, 23
McQueen. See M'Queen
Meldrum, --, 23
Meteiller, --, 17
Meteiller, Louis, 23
Meteller, --, 23
Meteyer, Louis, 06
Metier, --, 20
Millet, --, 20
Millet, John Babtiste, 12
Milliet, J. B., 22
Milliet, John Babtiste, 06
Mills, Thomas, 27
Minie, Francois, 06
Miny, Francis, 18

Mitchel, Joseph, 06
Mois, John Babtiste, 06
Monplaisir, --, 14
Monplesir, Andrez, 06
Monplesir, Andrez, 13
Montplesir, 16
Montplesir, Andrez, 10
Moreau, --, 12
Morrison, John, 26
Morrison, John, 28
Morrison, William, 26
Morrison, William, 28
Morrison, William, heirs of, 26
Myot, Nicholas, 12
Nangle, Andrew, 26
Neall, Michael, 11
Neau, --, 22
Neau, Michael, 06
Neau, Michael, 10
Nicholas, --, 16
Nicholas, --, 18
Noveaux, --, 24
Noyon, Toussant, 11
Ouilette, Alexis, 12
Ouilette, John Babtiste, 06
Ouillette, John Baptiste, 18
Page, --, 16
Page, --, 18
Page, --, 21
Page, --, 23
Page, William, 20
Page, William, 22
Pannah. See Renez Godere
Paquin, --, 15
Park, --, 23
Park, William, 21
Payes, Guillaume, 06
Pea, Henry, 27
Pea, Jacob, 18
Pecon, Peter, 12
Pelliere, Andrew, 13
Peltier, --, 19
Peltier, --, 22
Peltier, --, widow of, 15
Peltier, Felicite, widow of Francois Peltier, 07
Peltier, Louisa, widow of Andre Peltier, 07
Peret, Peter, 17
Perodeau, --, 22
Perodeau, Joseph, 06

Peron, Pier, 08
Perredeau, Joseph, 13
Perredeau, Joseph, the younger, 13
Perret, Peter, 19
Perret, Pierre 06
Perron, Amable, 06
Perrot, Mary Louis, widow of Nicholas Perrot, 07
Perrot, Nicholas, 23
Peter, --, 22
Petit, Antoine, 21
Philips, Henry, 26
Phillibert, Angelic, widow of Etienne Phillibert, 07
Plifford, --, 12
Popenoe, Peter, 26
Popenoe, Peter, 27
Popenoe, Peter, heirs of, 26
Proux, --, 11
Pyat, Benjamin, 26
Quenez, Pierre, Sr., 06
Queret, --, 13
Queret, --, 15
Queret, Peter, 13
Queret, Peter, 13
Querez, Peter, 19
Querre, Pierre, and wife, 28
Racine, --, 13
Racine, Andrew, 28
Racine, F. P. A., 17
Racine, Francois, 06
Racine, J. B., 17
Racine, John Babtiste St.-Marie, 06
Racine, John Baptiste, 17
Racine, Mary, 25
Racine, Pierre et Andrez, 07
Radley, John, 26
Radley. See Bradley
Ramsay, Allen, 16
Ranger, --, 19
Raperault, --, 12
Rapuault, --, 15
Raux, Joseph, 07
Raux, Joseph, 11
Ravalet, Jean Baptiste, 28
Ravalet, Louis, 07
Ravalet, Louis, 27
Ravalet, Louis, 28
Ravelet, Louise, 20
Read, --, 14
Reaux, --, 21

Redyente, --, 12
Regis, --, 10
Regnez, Pierre, 06
Richard, J. B., 13
Richard, John Baptiste, 15
Richard, Marie Josephe, 28
Richards, --, 16
Richarville, --, 21
Richarville, Antoine, 17
Riendo, --, 13
Rimbault, Pierre, Senior, 28
Robinson, Andrew, 26
Robinson, James, 28
Robison, James, 28
Roderigo, Diego, 28
Roi, --, 20
Roi, Andrez, 21
Roi, John Baptiste, 21
Roupiault, Louis, 07
Rouse, Joseph, 08
Roussiant, Francois, 09
Roy, Andre, 08
Roy, Andrez, 09
Sabolle, Joseph, 07
Saboulle, --, 15
Saint Ange. See St. Ange
Saint Aubin. See St. Aubin
Saint Jean. See St. Jean
Saint Marie. See St. Marie
Saint Martin. See St. Martin
Saint Pierre. See St. Pierre
Sanschagrin, --, 11
Sanschagrin, --, 12
Sanschagrin, --, 13
Sansosy, --, 11
Sargent, Winthrop, 05
Sargent, Winthrop, 08
Sargent, Winthrop, 10
Sargent, Winthrop, 24
Seguin; Louis (Laderoute), 27
Seguin, Louis, 16
Shiskey, --, 22
Sims, --, 23
Simson, --, 21
Sinnet, Richard, 26
Small, --, 14
Small, --, 17
Small, John, 21
Small, John, 22

Springer, Ann, 20
Squires, David, 26
St. Ange, --, 02
St. Ange, --, 02
St. Aubin, --, 14
St. Aubin, John Babtiste, 07
St. Aubin, John Baptiste, 18
St. Aubin, John Baptiste, 21
St. Aubin, John, 10
St. Aubin, Louis, 19
St. Jean, --, 12
St. Marie, --, 13
St. Marie, --, 18
St. Marie, --, heirs of, 22
St. Marie, Etienne, 07
St. Marie, Joseph, 07
St. Marie, Joseph, 17
St. Marie, Joseph, 17
St. Marie, Joseph, 21
St. Marie, Stephen, 12
St. Marie, Stephen, 15
St. Marie, Stephen, 21
St. Martin, Adamhar, 20
St. Martin, Adamher, 22
St. Martin, Adamher, 23
St. Pierre, 16
St. Marie, Francois, 09
Ste. Marie, Joseph, 27
Ste. Marie, Pierre, 25
Stone, Maudeline, widow of Joseph Stone, 07
Sucrot, --, 16
Sullivan, --, 18
Sullivan, --, 19
Sullivan, Daniel, 23
Sullivan, Daniel, 26
Thomas, James, 26
Thompson, Joseph, 27
Todd, J., 02
Todd, J., 03
Tongas, Joseph, 07
Tongas. See also Tougas
Tougas, --, 11
Tougas, John Baptiste, 24
Tougas, John, 22
Tougas, Joseph, 11
Tougas, Joseph, 27
Toujas, --, 19
Toulon, John, 12
Tranbulle, --, widow of, 13

```
Trudel, --, 13
Trudel, Francois, 07
Turdelle, --, 20
Turpin, Francois, 07
Turpin, Richard Francis, 17
Vachet, Francis, 14
Vachet, Francis, 14
Vachette, Francois, 07
Vallee, Alexander, 11
Vallez, --, 16
Vallez, Alexander, 07
Vallez, Alexander, 23
Vaudrey, --, 22
Vaudry, Antoine, 19
Vaudry, J. B., 21
Vaudry, John Baptiste, 18
Vaudrye, --, 12
Vaudrye, --, 13
Vaudrye, --, 14
Vaudrye, --, 17
Vaudrye, --, 20
Vaudrye, Antoine, 07
Vaudrye, J. B., the younger, 15
Vaudrye, John Babtiste, 07
Vaudrye, John Babtiste, Jr., 07
Vigo, --, 13
Vigo, --, 19
Vigo, --, 19
Vigo, --, 19
Vigo, --, 23
Vigo, --, Major, 06
Vigo, Francis, 07
Vigo, Francis, 15
Vigo, M., 13
Vigo, M., 14
Villeneuve, --, 20
Villeneuve, Charles, 19
Villeneuve, Charles, 19
Villeneuve, Gennevieve, 19
Villenueve, --, 15
Villeray, --, 17
Villeraye, John Baptiste, 20
Vilray, John Babtiste, 07
Vogel. See Bogle
Walls, James, 12
Watts, --, 21
Watts, --, 23
Wilkes, Joseph, 26
Wilson, Thomas, 26
```

Wilson, Thomas, 27
Worthington, James, 26
Worthington, William, 26
Wyant, --, 18
Wyant, Christopher, 26
Wyant, Jacob, 26

Selections from **The American State Papers,** No. 2

French and British Land Grants in the

Post Vincennes (Indiana) District

1750-1784
(Continued)

Clifford Neal Smith

First printing, August 1996   rz
Reprint, November 1996   qz

FOREWORD

The American State Papers are official public documents printed privately long before the Congressional Printing Office existed. The printing of public documents during the very early Congresses was done without any general provision of law as to what should be printed. Even as early as 1829 the clerk of the House of Representatives reported that, for the period 1793-1803 not a vestige of manuscript and only a scattered few printed copies were extant. A contributing factor was the destruction of the Capitol building in 1814 by fire.

In 1821 a bill was passed which authorized the publication of 750 copies of all the documents that could be found. The documents were published by two private companies: Gales and Seaton, and Duff Green. Of the two publications, Gales and Seaton is the larger. The Duff Green collection of documents are less comprehensive than the Gales and Seaton collection, and there are many differences in the pagination, particularly in later volumes.

Both publishers appear to have divided the original documents into general subject categories: Foreign Affairs, Indian Affairs, Finance, Commerce and Navigation, Military Affairs, Naval Affairs, Post Office Department, Public Land, and Claim. For genealogical and family history researchers, the last two categories--Public Land and Claims--are the most valuable, and it is from these two categories that this monograph *Selections from* **The American State Papers** will be made. The Public Land category, in eight volumes, covers the period 1789-1837; the Claims category, in one volume, covers the period 1790-1823.

In 1972 an attempt was made to index all names in the Public Land and Claims categories of the American State Papers; the index, although monumental, is, however, not complete. All researchers are urged to read pages i through xxvii of

Phillip McMullin, editor, *Grassroots of America: A Computerized Index to the American State Papers: Land Grants and Claims (1789-1837) with Other Aids to Research* (Salt Lake City, Utah: Gendex Corporation, 1972).

The present *Selections from the American State Papers* are the selections, by narrower subject matter, from the Gales and Seaton edition, made by this compiler for the use of genealogists and family historians because the original volumes are now very rare and, no doubt, inaccessible to most researchers.

Cases not embraced by any act of Congress
(ASP 8:1:301)

No. 1. The United States' Wabash and Illinois Land Companies claim a tract of land, lying between the mouth of a rivuet emptying into the Wabash river, about thirty-two leagues above Vincennes, and a place called Pointe Coupee, about twelve leagues above the said village, extending forty leagues eastward, and thirty leagues westward of the Wabash. Another tract of the same dimensions, from east to west, between the mouth of White river and the mouth of the Wabash. Both said tracts conveyed to **Louis Viviat**, for himself and associates, by deed signed by a number of the Piankeshaw Indians, therein called chiefs and sachems of the Piankashaw nation of Indians, dated 18th October, 1785.

As a small part of the abovesaid tracts lies within the district of Vincennes, the commissioners are under the necessity of taking notice of the claim.

It appears to the commissioners that this purchase was a private transaction between the Indians and an individual, in direct violation of the King of Great Britain, dated 7th October, 1763, and, consequently illegal. And as no provisions are made to say of the laws of the United States for claims of this nature, the commissioners reject them.

No. 2. The French inhabitants of Vincennes claim a tract of twenty-four leagues square, joining the two tracts claimed by the Illinois and Wabash Land Companies. The only evidence in support of this claim is a reservation contained in the abovementioned deed, from the Indians, of the intermediate space between the above two tracts, for the use of the inhabitants of Vincennes. This reservation can be no more than the manifestation of the intention of the Indians to make the grant, and cannot be considered as a real transfer. But, admitting it was, the deed itself being illegal and void, the claim must be rejected.

No. 3. *Upper Prairie*--The several persons to whom or to whose assigns the several tract of the upper prairie have been confirmed, (as will more fully appear by reference to a map of the prairie, (Document 1) wherein the name of the respective claimants are inserted,) have claimed the several tracts contained within the lines AB, BC, and elm road CD, DK, the line KI, and the Wabash, known by the denomination of continuation, held under Indian deeds and in quiet possession of the several owners thereof, for at least twenty-five years.

[Document 1 (ASP:8:1:302)

2.

Plan of the Ancient possessions of the Upper Prairie confirmed by the Governors, their continuation from the Elm road to the Wabash and Indian field]

[Names mentioned therein are:

Nicholas Chapard, Henry Vandenburgh, Heirs of Pierre Cornoyer, Heirs of Nicholas Cardinal, Joseph Barren, Heirs of Paul Gamelin, Francois Vigo, Heirs of Jean B[aptis]te Du Chesne, Robert Buntin, William Harrison]

The original titles to the several tracts here alluded to, being derived from Indian purchases unauthorized by law, the Governors have refused to act upon such claims, under the impression that those cases did not come within the powers delegated to them; and the commissioners being of the same opinion, with regard to the authority vested in them, refer the whole to Congress, the only competent tribunal to decide thereon.

The will, however, observe that the present claimants may plead the same length of possession, by which Congress was induced to grant, by section 3d of the act of March, 1791, the Indian fields to the several possessors thereof, and beg leave to suggest the propriety of legislative interference.

N.B. The contents of the several tracts alluded to above, and claimed as continuation, amount, in the whole, to two hundred and forty-three acres and one hundred and one perches.

No. 4. The heirs of **Francois Bosseron** and **Ambrose Dagenet** claim an uncertain quantity of land, by a grant from the court to **Francois Bosseron** and **Ambrose Dagenet**, dated November 20th, 1783; beginning on the northwest side of the Wabash, opposite Pointe Coupee, about three miles from the Wabash; thence, running at right angles with the Wabash, until it strikes the river Embarras; thence, down the said river Embarrass, to within three miles west of the Wabash; thence up the said Wabash, and parallel with the several courses thereof, at the distance of three miles therefrom, to the place of beginning; granted by order of **Nicholas Perrott, Pierre Gamelin**, and **Pierre Querre**, magistrates, and signed by **Gabriel Legrand**, clerk of the court.

Thomas Flower claims an undivided third part of an undivided seventh part of the above entire grant, as assignee of the heirs of the aforesaid **Francois Bosseron**.

Thomas Flower, assignee of **Ambrose Dagenet** and -- **Bosseron**, claims an uncertain quantity, part of the abovesaid grant.

Thomas Flower claims an undivided third part of an undivided fourth part of a grant made by the court to **Pierre Querre**, son, of a tract beginning at the river Marie, to White river, and about ten leagues deep; excluding from the said grant any land they may been already granted, to **Pierre Querre**, father.

The heirs of **Isaac Decker**, assignee of **Pierre Querre**, father, claim two thousand acres, part of the preceding grant.

Jonathan Purcell, assignee of **Pierre Querre**, father, claims five thousand acres, part of the same grant.

Thomas Flower, assignee of **Pierre Querre**, claims twenty thousand acres, part of the same grant.

Thomas Flower claims an uncertain quantity, as assignee of the said **Pierre Querre**.

Thomas Flower claims an undivided third part of an undivided moiety of an entire grant from the court to **Pierre Gamelin** and **Nicholas Perrott**, dated 20th November, 1783, lying between Pointe Coupee and river Marie, two leagues deep excluding from the said grant any land that may have been already granted, as assignee to **Pierre Gamelin**.

Thomas Flower, as assignee of **Pierre Gamelin**, claims forty-one thousand acres, part of the proceeding grant.

Jonathan Purcell, assignee of **Pierre Gamelin** and **Nicholas Perrott**, claim twenty-seven thousand five hundred acres, part of the foregoing grant.

William Purcell, assignee of **Pierre Gamelin** and **Nicholas Perrott**, claims one thousand acres, part of the same grant.

Andrew Purcell, assignee of **Pierre Gamelin** and **Nicholas Perrott**, claims one thousand acres, part of the same grant.

Without dwelling on the extraordinary circumstances of the above rejected supposed grants, wherein the members of a court of justice have made to each with unusual donations, and appropriated to themselves such a large and valuable part of the country, the commissioners will observe that the State of Virginia never authorized the courts to grant lands. That after the cession, Congress, taking into consideration the hard case of a number of inhabitants, who, under the impressions that these grants were good, had moved into Vincennes and the Illinois country, benevolently stepped in, by the act of 1791, and directed the Governors of the territory to confirm claims of that description, provided the land claimed had been actually improved and cultivated, not exceeding four hundred acres to a person. Considering, therefore, the present claims as grounded upon a transaction fraudulent *ab initio*, entirely unusual, (the same court never having before granted more than four hundred arpents or three hundred and forty acres, with a clause of actual settlement thereto annexed,) and not contemplated by the act of 1791, reject, *in toto*, all the foregoing claims.

H.
Special Cases
[ASP 8:1:301]

Amongst the claims contained in Judge **[Henry] Vanderburgh's** notice, entered on the first day of January, 1801, as settled, and written in his own hand, is to be found the following, viz.

A. "28, one other tract of one hundred and sixty arpents, joining the two last mentioned tracts, confirmed and ordered to be surveyed by order of the Governor of the territory, for **Angelique Racine**, only heir of **Jean Baptiste Racine**, called **Beauchain**, her father, and by the same **Angelique [Racine]** and **L. Denoyon**, her husband, assigned to the said **Henry Vanderburgh**."

To which is annexed the following general certificate, written in the same hand, and signed by the Secretary of the Indian territory:

Secretary's Office, December 31, 1804.

B. "I, **John Gibson**, Secretary of the Indiana territory, do certify that I have carefully examined the foregoing claims to land, from number to number thirty-four inclusive, the property of **Henry Vanderburgh**, Esq., and that they have all been confirmed and ordered to be surveyed by the different Governors of the territory, as appears on record in the said office. Given under my hand at Vincennes, the day and date above written.

John Gibson, Secretary Indiana Territory."

The same **Henry Vanderburgh** entered on the same day a notice written and signed by him, with the name **Angelique Racine**, in the words following, viz.

C. "Notice to, etc. of the land claimed by **Angelique Racine**, as heir to her father, **Jean Baptiste Racine, dit Beauchain**.

"A tract of one hundred and sixty arpents, confirmed and ordered to be surveyed by the Governor of the territory, a certified copy of which is herewith delivered."

Enclosed in the above notice, and in support of the last and foregoing claims, was the following certificate in the name **Henry Vanderburgh**'s handwriting, except the words "alias Beauchain," and signed by the Secretary of the territory.

D. "I certify that there is an order of the Governor of the territory in my office, to survey for **Angelique Racine**, as heir of her father, **Jean Baptiste Racine**, one hundred and sixty arpents of land. Also, one other tract for one hundred and sixty arpents of land to the said **Angelique Racine**, as heir to her said father, **Jean Baptiste Racine**, alias **Beauchain**.

John Gibson, Secretary of Indiana Territory."

Underneath the said certificate is written, in the same handwriting, as follows, viz. "One of the above tracts has been conveyed to **Henry Vanderburgh**, and is entered with his claim."

In the record of **Winthrop Sargent**'s entries of claims to land, made in 1797, book B, are found the following entries, respectively numbered by number fifty-one and one hundred and twenty-nine, in the handwriting of the said **Henry Vanderburgh**:

E. "**Angelique Racine**, four arpents by forty at the Big Hill, which was granted and allotted to her father, **Francois Racine**, upwards of thirty years ago. **Pierre Cartier** and **Jean Baptiste Potevin** prove the grant, allotment, and cultivation, in which they aided, in company with the said **[Francois] Racine**. The land is three miles east of the village, or thereabouts. -- **Decotteaux** also proves the above."

F. "The heirs of **Jean Baptiste [Racine dit] Beauchain**, one of the first settlers of this country, claim one hundred and sixty arpents of land joining the donation. The land has been called for more than forty years -- **Beauchain**, cote, after the owner's name. This land, from the best information, though not positively proven, seems to have been assigned him by the Governor of this place, upwards of forty years ago. The claim, therefore, appears to have gained strength from its great antiquity; and, from this consideration, we are induced to recommend it to your particular attention. **Beauchain** died in the country, and never owned any other land."

When these claims were exhibited, **Henry Vanderburgh** was acting with others, as commissioners, to receive land claims, by appointment of Colonel **[Winthrop] Sargent.**

In consequence of the foregoing entries, the following orders of survey were issued, as recorded in **Winthrop Sargent's** book C, containing warrants of survey, pages 24 and 34:

G. "**Angelique Racine**, four arpents by forty, at the Big Hill; granted and allotted to her father **Francois Racine**, upwards of thirty years ago, about three miles eastward of Vincennes."

H. "The heirs of **Jean Baptiste [Racine dit] Beauchain** one hundred and sixty arpents of land, joining the donation. Survey the same, agreeably to ancient boundaries, it appearing to have been very early in the family."

The first order of survey, marked G, is not executed; the land being included in the donation tract, is located on the west side of the Wabash, and is alluded to in the entry C, of **Angelique Racine**, who therein calls her father **Jean Baptiste Racine**, and not **Francois [Racine]**.

The second order of survey H, has been executed; the land surveyed, in consequence thereof, lies, some distance south from the donation tract, and is alluded to in the entry A of **Henry Vanderburgh**, the present claimant, where he called **Angelique Denoyon's** father **Jean Baptiste Racine, alias Beauchain.** That the father of **Angelique Racine** should be named by the same person in one place, A and C, **Jean Baptiste Racine dit Beauchain**, in another, G, **Francois Racine**, and in a third, H and F, **Jean Baptiste Beauchain**, were circumstances calculated to awaken suspicion, inasmuch as **Henry Vanderburgh** is son-in-law of **Angelique Racine**, formerly Mrs. **Cornoyer**, now Mrs. **Denoyon**, and could not be supposed to mistake the name of the father of his wife's mother.

The Secretary of the territory, to whom these suspicions were communicated, went into an examination of the books of Colonel **[Winthrop] Sargent**, and sent to the commissioners the following letter, to which was prefixed the two orders of survey, marked G and H, verbatim, as they stand on Colonel **[Winthrop] Sargent's** record, properly certified and subscribed by him.

To the Commissioners of the Land Office for the district of Vincennes.

"Gentlemen:

"On the 26th of December, 1804, I signed a certificate, of which the following is a copy," viz. [Here follows the certificate alluded to, inserted above, and marked D.] "This certificate was given at the solicitation of Judge -- **Vanderburgh**, who assisted me, as Secretary of the territory, to compare the contents thereof with the original record in my office. I have since found that it was not conformable to the record, but that the confirmation to the two tracts of land therein mentioned, made by Colonel -- **Sargent**, were in the words and figures first above written (see G and H.) As the former certificate is erroneous, and done this mistake, I beg you will make the necessary alterations therein, as it may comport with the original record. I am, gentlemen, etc.

John Gibson, Secretary Indiana Territory."

With a view to throw some light on a subject involved in such obscurity, the commissioners examined **Francois Racine**, son of the late commandant, who, upon his oath, made the following answers to a series of questions put to him by the commissioners:

That the name of **Angelique Racine**'s father was **Francois Racine**, called Beauchene.

That the name of his own father was **Jean Baptiste Racine**, called, for distinction sake, **Ste. Marie**, formerly commandant under the British Government in this place. That **Francois Racine** never was called **Jean Baptiste [Racine?]**.

That the hill above **Abraham F. Snapp**'s mill was called the Grand Cote a' Beauchene, and was one and the same place; that he never knew a man by the name of **Jean Baptiste Beauchain**.

From which it appears evident that a grant of one hundred and thirty-six acres (one hundred and sixty arpents) was made to **Angelique Racine**, in right of her father, Francois at the Grand Cote, the Big Hill: that the union of the christian name **Jean Baptiste Racine, alias Ste. Marie**, and making the Big Hill and Cote a' Beauchene, which are one and the same spot, two different places, a second grant has been obtained for a person who never had existence. That the two notices entered by Judge -- **Vanderburgh**, for himself, as assignee of **Angelique Cornoyer** or **Denoyon**, in right of her father **Jean Baptiste Racine alias Beauchene**, for one hundred and thirty-six acres, and by for the same **Angelique [Racine]**, in the same right, for a similar quantity, tally only with the certificate surreptitiously obtained from General -- **Gibson**, and not with the record of **Winthrop Sargent**, mentioned above.

The commissioners are, therefore, of opinion, that the grant made to **Angelique Racine**, as heir to her father **Francois [Racine]** ought to be confirmed, although her notice is incorrect, in claiming in the name of **Jean Baptiste [Racine]** instead of **Francois [Racine]**, her real father, and it is entered as such in the list of confirmed claims.

That the Governor's grant to the heirs of **Jean Baptiste Beauchene** ought to be considered a nullity, as having been made to an ideal person, under a feigned name, made use of for the purpose of deceiving the Governor.

That **Henry Vanderburgh**, the present claimant, cannot be considered as an innocent purchaser, as the whole transaction, from the beginning, has been conducted by him, and in his own handwriting, and that the land surveyed for the heirs of **Jean Baptiste Beauchene** still belongs to the United States.

No. 2. Judge **[Henry] Vanderburgh** entered his claim to one hundred acres of land, part of a donation tract, as assignee of **Joseph Hamelin**, to whom claimant says the same was granted as head of a family at Vincennes, before the year 1783.

John Harbin has laid claim to the remaining three hundred acres, as assignee of the said **Joseph Hamelin**.

In the records of the territory is found the grant of four hundred acres to one **Joseph Hamelin**, to whom No. 88 of said donation tract was allotted, now claimed by **Richard Pollard**, as assignee, (Document B.) and but one **Joseph Hamelin** is to be found on the record. The only support of the present claim is an order of survey from **Arthur St. Clair**, directed to **Robert Buntin**, Surveyor of the Public Lands, found amongst the papers, whereof the following is a copy. (See book B, page 250.)

"Survey for **Joseph Hamelin**, four hundred acres of land, a donation as a head of family, contiguous to the donation tract, it having been proven to me that he is entitled as head of a family, in 1783, but his name omitted when the list was made ut, and this shall be your warrant.

[signed] **A. St. Clair**

[To:] **Robert Buntin, Esq.**, Surveyor of Knox.
December 21, 1790."

The fact stated in the above order of survey, namely, that **Joseph Hamelin**'s name had been omitted when the list was made out, is evidently a mistake, since, from the records of the territory, it appears that a donation tract was in fact granted to one **Joseph Hamelin**, who drew No. 88. They, therefore, reject these claims as founded on the above order of survey. It remained, then, for the commissioners to consider this case as unsettled on the presumption that there existed another man of the same name, who might have been entitled; but of this they have obtained no evidence.

No. 3. **James Legerwood**, assignee of **William Page**, three hundred and forty acres, by a grant of the court, dated 10th March 1782.

The only support of this claim which has been entered, and considered by claimant as settled, is an authenticated copy of the deed of the court to **William Page**, of the abovementioned number of acres, on Mill creek, with the following words, evidently in Governor **St. Clair**'s handwriting, viz. "to be surveyed," endorsed on the back thereof which copy was forwarded to Governor -- **Harrison**, in the fall, 1804, together with sundry other papers and petitions, with annotations in the same handwriting, appearing to have been memoranda of the said Governor's decisions thereon. These papers were handed by Governor -- **Harrison** to the Register. No confirmation of the same claim appears in the records of the territory. In addition to the above, it is to be observed that the land herein claimed has been two or three years in the possession of the claimant, a bona fide purchaser, who lives and has made valuable improvements thereon. The commisssioners, without any evidence of cultivation and improvement, would have rejected this claim; but being induced to believe that it had been confirmed by Governor -- **St. Clair**, although by him neglected to be entered on the territorial records, have come to a determination to consider this claim as confirmed, and have entered the same on their books accordingly.

No. 4: **Francois Hamelin** and **Pierre Cabassier** have entered in the Register's office their respective claims to donation rights, as heads of families at Cahokia, and have exhibited affidavits in support thereof.

The above claims may have been entered with the Register of the Kaskaskia district: that consideration alone would justify the commissioners in declining to take them up.

But they are convinced that they have no power to enter into the investigation of claims which do not belong in their district, and therefore, decline expressing any opinion on their merits.

(ASP 8:1:303)

Vincennes, 20th September 1806

Sir:

I do myself the honor of addressing you on a subject which, to me, is of the most interesting nature. The very extraordinary report, made by **Nathaniel Ewing** and **John Badollet**, Esquires, Commissioners of the Land Office for the District of Vincennes, respecting two tracts of land of one hundred and sixty arpents each, granted by **Winthrop Sargent**, acting as Governor of the territory in the year 1797, one of the heirs of **Jean Baptiste Beauchene**, and the other to **Angelique Racine**, heir to her father **Francois Racine**, was never communicated to me, until the morning of the second instant, and then in a very confidential manner by **Henry Hunt**, clerk of the general court of the territory, at whose house both the commissioners lived during the whole time they were engaged in this transaction. I was never notified in any way whatsoever to produce any testimony, which might have explained and done away the doubts and difficulties which they allege exist. Nor was I ever present, or had the least knowledge of any testimony which they examined on the subject. Since this transaction has come to my knowledge, I have been much occupied in the general court, and have, therefore, delayed making you this communication until today. I now take the liberty of soliciting you to suspend any opinion on the report, and not to expose it to the view of any person, until I can forward such papers, documents, and testimony, as shall prove, I trust, satisfactory to yourself, as well as to the committee of Congress before whom these papers are to be laid. It is probably they will be sent on by Mr. -- **Park**, the delegate of this territory.

I am, with the greatest respect and regard, sir, your most obedient, humble servant.

[Signed] **Henry Vanderburgh**

[To:] **Albert Gallatin**, Esq.

Supplement to A and C

A.

List of lands confirmed by the different Governors, in virtue of French or British Grants, and of court and commandant deeds
(ASP 8:1:559)

Claimants:
 Original: **Astrus, alias Guiguvlet, Alexis**
 Present: **Jeremiah Mayes**
50 acres, surveyed; between Des Chis and White river, bounded by **William Reed, Peter Frederick**, and vacant lands.

Claimants:
 Original: Asturgas, Minor
 Present: **Minor Asturgas, heirs of**
340.44 acres, surveyed; on river Des Chis, bounded by **Mich[ael] Thorn, J. R. Jones, Benj[amin] Beckes**, and others.

Claimants:
 Original: **Asturgas, Minor**
 Present: **Minor Asturgas**, heirs **of**
59.16 acres, surveyed; on Bosseron creek, bounded by **Frederick Berger, James Ledgerwood**, and others.

Claimants:
 Original: **Addison, William**
 Present: **Louis N. Fortin**
300 acres, surveyed; on waters of Wilson's creek, joining No. 12, additional donation

Claimants:
 Original: **Ardrine, L.**
 Present: **John Westfall**
50 acres, surveyed; on southeast side of White river; joining **P. Catt.**

Claimants:
 Original: **Aschar, Joseph**
 Present: **William Bullett**
50 acres, not surveyed.

Claimants:
 Original: **Arpin, Jean Baptiste**
 Present: **Thomas Melton**
200 acres, surveyed; on White river, joining the additional donation below, and joining the mouth of a small creek.

Claimants:
 Original: **Askin, John**
 Present: **John Askin**
 68.16 acres, surveyed; on northwest side Wabash.

Claimants:
 Original: **Barril, Francois**
 Present: **Laurent Bazadone**
 50 acres, not surveyed.

Claimants:
 Original: **Bondy, Antoine**
 Present: **Daniel Smith**
 136.16 acres, surveyed; above the Little Rock, on the Wabash, joining **Paul Gamelin**.

Claimants:
 Original: **Berger, Frederick**
 Present: **John Pea**
 136.16 acres, surveyed; on waters of river Des Chis, bounded.

Claimants:
 Original: **Boyer, Francois**
 Present: **Adam Harness**
 50 acres, surveyed; on southeast side of Wabash, below the Little Rock, joining **Jacques Rough**.

Claimants:
 Original: **Bosseron, Francois**
 Present: **Abner Reeves, heirs of**
 340.44 acres, surveyed; on northwest side of Wabash, bounded by **A. F. Snapp** and the Wabash.

Claimants:
 Original: **Antoine Bordeleau**
 Present: **Antoine Bordeleau, heirs of**
 68.24 acres, surveyed; in Cathelinette Prairie, bounded by **Charles Lefevre** and **Rene Langlois**.

Claimants:
 Original: **Beckes, Benjamin**
 Present: **Benjamin Beckes**
 200 acres, surveyed; on river Des Chis, bounded by **Minard Asturgas**.

Claimants:
Original: **Beckes, Benjamin**
Present: **Benjamin Beckes**
200 acres, surveyed; on river Des Chis, adjoining his tract of 340 acres, in right of **Moses Carter**.

Claimants:
Original: **Beckes, Benjamin**
Present: **Benjamin Beckes**
100 acres, surveyed; on river Des Chis, adjoining his tract of 200 acres, **Luke Decker**, **R. Johnson**, and **R. Sturgiss**.

Claimants:
Original: **Beckes, Benjamin**
Present: **Benjamin Beckes**
126 acres, surveyed; in the lower prairie, bounded by **F. Vigo**.

Claimants:
Original: **Bolon, Hypolite**
Present: **David Price**
200 acres, surveyed; on waters of Marie creek, joining said -- Price.

Claimants:
Original: **Bonhomme, Jean Baptiste**
Present: **Benjamin D. Price**
272 acres, surveyed; on waters of Marie creek, joining other lands of said **B[enjamin] D. Price**.

Claimants:
Original: **Barrackman, Henry**
Present: **Jacob Plough**
100 acres, surveyed; on the southeast side of Wabash, opposite the Little Rock, joining -- **Harness**.

Claimants:
Original: **Berger, Peter**
Present: **David Crock**
100 acres, surveyed; on White river, joining **Al. Ramsay**.

Claimants:
Original: **Berger, Peter**
Present: **Heirs of Isaac Decker**
50 acres, surveyed; on south side of White river, joining other lands of said Decker.

Claimants:
 Original: **Beedle, Elias**
 Present: **Samuel Johnston**
 200 acres, surveyed; in forks of Marie creek, joining **A. Wilkins**.

Claimants:
 Original: **Bosseron, Francois**
 Present: **-- Dubois & -- Marchall**
 136.16 acres, surveyed; on northwest side of Wabash, joining **John Askins** and **M. Brouillette**.

Claimants:
 Original: **Binette, Jean Baptiste**
 Present: **Antoine Marchall**
 64.140 acres, surveyed; in the lower prairie, joining -- **Dagneau** and **P. Derousse**.

Claimants:
 Original: **Binette, Jean Baptiste**
 Present: **Vital Boucher**
 40.130 acres, surveyed; in the lower prairie, joining -- **Dagneau** and **P. Derousse**.

Claimants:
 Original: **Bolon, Amable**
 Present: **Abraham F. Snapp**
 50 acres, surveyed; on Small's creek.

Claimants:
 Original: **Barrackman, Peter**
 Present: **Peter Barrackman, heirs of**
 170.27 acres; surveyed; on river Des Chis, Barrackman's station.

Claimants:
 Original: **Bordeleau, Michel, heirs of -- Decointre**
 Present: **Jacob Pea**
 50 acres, not surveyed.

Claimants:
 Original: **Berger, Frederick, Jun[ior]**
 Present: **Heirs of Frederick Berger**
 300 acres, surveyed; on the high ground between Marie and Bosseron creeks, joining said -- **Berger**, **J. Ledgerwood**, and -- **Black**.

Claimants:
 Original: **Berger, Frederick, Sen[ior]**
 Present: **Frederick Berger, Sen[ior]**
 300 acres, surveyed; on the high ground, between Marie and Bosseron creeks, joining -- **Black**.

Claimants:
 Original: **Boyer, Francois**
 Present: **Francis Williams**
 50 acres, surveyed; on the high ground, between Marie and Bosseron [creeks?], joining other lands of said -- **Williams**.

Claimants:
 Original: **Boucher, Vital**
 Present: **William H. Harrison**
 87.48 acres, surveyed; in the upper prairie.

Claimants:
 Original: **Bosseron, Francois**
 Present: **William H. Harrison**
 136.16 acres, surveyed; on the north side of Wabash, joining other lands of said Harrison.

Claimants:
 Original: **Baily, John**
 Present: **William H. Harrison**
 136.16 acres, surveyed; on the north side of Wabash, joining other lands of Harrison.

Claimants:
 Original: **Bordeleau, Antoine**
 Present: **Jeremiah Claypole**
 50 acres, not surveyed.

Claimants:
 Original: **Bolon, Louis**
 Present: **Jeremiah Claypole**
 50 acres, not surveyed.

(ASP 8:1:560)

Claimants:
 Original: **Bosseron, Francois**
 Present: **Toussaint Dubois**
 50 acres, surveyed; on southeast side of White river, joining other lands of Dubois.

Claimants:
 Original: **Bosseron, Francois**
 Present: [**Toussaint**] **Dubois**
 340.44 acres, surveyed; on southeast side of White river, joining heirs of **John Glass** and other lands of said Dubois.

Claimants:
 Original: **Bergand, Charles**
 Present: **Toussaint Dubois**
 34 acres, [not surveyed.]

Claimants:
 Original: **Bergeron, Louis**
 Present: **Toussaint Dubois**
 50 acres, surveyed; on Embarras river, joining other lands of said Dubois.

Claimants:
 Original: **Bazinette, Francois**
 Present: **Toussaint Dubois**
 50 acres, surveyed; located below the mouth of Natte river, on northwest side Wabash, adjoining other lands of said Dubois.

Claimants:
 Original: **Boyer, Toussaint**
 Present: **George Wallace, Jun[ior]**
 50 acres, surveyed; [survey location not given].

Claimants:
 Original: **Barrackman, Peter**, heirs of, assignee of **Andre Languedoc**
 Present: same
 50 acres, surveyed; [survey location not given].

Claimants:
 Original: **Beauchain, Jean Baptiste**, heirs of
 Present: United States (*vide* Special Report)
 136 acres, surveyed; on Mill creek, johning **R. Buntin**, **F. Vigo**.

Claimants:
 Original: **Barrackman, Peter**, heirs of
 Present: **George Wallace**
 200 acres, not surveyed.

Claimants:
 Original: **Boyer, Peter**
 Present: **Susan Sullivan**
Acreage not surveyed; in Cathelinette prairie; quantity not mentioned.

Claimants:
 Original: **Bosseron, --**
 Present: **Jean Baptiste Laplante**
59.80 acres, surveyed; on the northwest side the Wabash, joining.

Claimants:
 Original: **Bergand, Dominique**
 Present: **William McIntosh**
68 acres, not surveyed; five miles below Vincennes, joining **N. Chapard**.

Claimants:
 Original: **Bono, Nicholas**
 Present: **William McIntosh**
50 acres, surveyed; at the grand rapids on the west side the Wabash.

Claimants:
 Original: **Boyer, Louis**
 Present: **Henry Vanderburgh**
68 acres, surveyed; in upper prairie joining.

Claimants:
 Original: **Bosseron, Francois**
 Present: **Henry Vanderburgh**
5.16 acres, not surveyed; in the Indian fields, joining Vincennes.

Claimants:
 Original: **Borneau, Charles**
 Present: **Jean F. Hamtramck**, heirs of
68 acres, surveyed; in lower prairie, joining -- **Villenaive** and -- **Mallett**.

Claimants:
 Original: **Baillarjon, Nicholas**
 Present: **Nicholas Baillarjon**, heirs of
68 acres, surveyed; in the prairie of the Grand Marsh, joining **P. Goder** and -- **Vaudry**.

Claimants:
 Original: **Barthe, Pierre**
 Present: **Robert Buntin**
 68.8 acres, surveyed; on northwest side Wabash, joining heirs of **P. Gamelin** and **T. Jones**.

Claimants:
 Original: **Brouillette, Michel**
 Present: **Robert Buntin**
 340.40 acres, not surveyed.

Claimants:
 Original: **Binette, Jean Baptiste**
 Present: **Simon Gonzalis**
 200 acres, not surveyed; located on Embarras, at or near the black ground, joining.

Claimants:
 Original: **Bergeron, Louis, the original grantee, J. B. Chartier**
 Present: **Francis Vigo**
 68 acres, not surveyed; granted, on northwest side of Wabash, joining other lands of said Vigo.

Claimants:
 Original: **Berger, George**
 Present: **John R. Jones**
 150 acres, surveyed; on White river, joining **J. Decker**.

Claimants:
 Original: **Berger, George**
 Present: **George Berger**, heirs of
 150 acres, surveyed; on White river, joining **J. Decker**.

Claimants:
 Original: **Bosseron, Francois**
 Present: **John R. Jones**
 136.16 acres, not surveyed.

Claimants:
 Original: **Bosseron, Francois**
 Present: **John R. Jones**
 136.16 acres, not surveyed.

Claimants:
 Original: **Boyer, Louis**
 Present: **Christopher Wyant**
 50 acres, illegally surveyed; [no location].

Claimants:
Original: **Barrackman, Christopher**
Present: **Christopher Barrackman**, heirs of
200 acres, not surveyed.

Claimants:
Original: **Barrackman, Abraham**
Present: **Abraham Barrackman**
150 acres, not surveyed.

Claimants:
Original: **Bonneau, Charles, Sen[ior]**
Present: **Henry Pea**
50 acres, not surveyed.

Claimants:
Original: **Bosseron, Jean Baptiste**
Present: **Benjamin Bullett**
136.16 acres, surveyed; on the northwest side of the wabash, joining **Robert Bantin** and **S. Baird**.

Claimants:
Original: **Bordeleau, Jean Baptiste**
Present: **Joshua Harbin**, heirs of
136.16 acres, surveyed; on the river Des Chis, joining other lands of said heirs.

Claimants:
Original: **Chabert, --**, widow of
Present: **Vital Boucher**, and her heirs
105.16 acres, surveyed; in the lower prairie.

Claimants:
Original: **Coder, Pierre**, widow of
Present: **Francis Racicos**
80.54 acres, surveyed; in the lower prairie, bounded by **Nicholas Byerjeon**, and **M. Bordeleau**.

Claimants:
Original: **Cardinal, Jean Baptiste**
Present: **Adam Harness**
50 acres, surveyed; on southeast side of Wabash, at the little rock, joining **Jacob Plough**.

Claimants:
 Original: **Carter, Moses**
 Present: **Benjamin Beckes**
 340 acres, surveyed; on river Des Chis, joining his other tracts.

Claimants:
 Original: **Carmichael, James**
 Present: **Ephraim Jordan**
 150 acres, not surveyed.

Claimants:
 Original: **Charbonneau, Jacques**
 Present: **Thomas Holder**
 50 acres, surveyed; on waters of Bosseron, joining **James Ledgerwood**.

Claimants:
 Original: **Coder, Rene, Jun[ior]**
 Present: **Abraham Kuykindall**
 50 acres, surveyed; on White river, joining the folowing tract of said Kuykindall.

Claimants:
 Original: **Chartier, Joseph**
 Present: **Abraham Kuykindall**
 204 acres, surveyed; on White river, joining other lands of said Kuykindall.

Claimants:
 Original: **Cardinal, Jacques**
 Present: **Patrick Simpson**
 102.12 acres, surveyed; on southeast of the upper prairie lots, joining **J. Latrimouille** and **W. Reed**.

Claimants:
 Original: **Caty, Antoine**
 Present: **Antoine Caty**
 112 acres, surveyed; in the lower prairie, joining widow -- **Leveron**.

Claimants:
 Original: **Caty, Antoine**, heirs of
 Present: **Jacob Pea**
 50 acres, not surveyed.

Claimants:
 Original: **Catt, Phillip**
 Present: **Phillip Catt**
 300 acres, surveyed; on southeast of White river, including the forks of Conger's creek, joining other lands of said Catt.

(ASP 8:1:561)

Claimants:
 Original: **Chapart, Nicholas**
 Present: **Chapart, Nicholas, heirs of**
 68.24 acres, surveyed; in the lower prairie, joining **Ray** and **L. Mallett**, No. 14.

Claimants:
 Original: **Chapart, Nicholas**
 Present: **Nicholas Chapart,** heirs of
 68 acres, not surveyed; granted, below the lower prairie, joining heirs of **Dominique Bergand.**

Claimants:
 Original: **Cardide, Jean**
 Present: **James Johnson,** Esq.
 180 acres, surveyed; on Mill creek, joining said -- **Johnson,** General -- **Gibson,** and others.

Claimants:
 Original: **Coder, Andre**
 Present: **William H. Harrison**
 118.145 acres, surveyed; below the lower prairie, on the Wabash, joining **A Montplaisir** and **W. Page.**

Claimants:
 Original: **Chartier Debeauch, Joseph**
 Present: **Frederick Lindey**
 50 acres, surveyed; on waters of river Des Chis, joining **S.** and **L. Frederick,** and vacant lands.

Claimants:
 Original: **Chapard, Nicholas, Jun[ior]**
 Present: **Nicholas Chapard, Jun[ior],** heirs of
 68.16 acres, surveyed in part; granted, below the lower prairie, to be resurveyed for a full quantity.

Claimants:
 Original: **Coder, Francois***
 Present: **Francis* Coder,** heirs of (*so spelled)
 136.16 acres, not surveyed; granted, at the Horse-shoe swamp, south of the lower prairie, at the end of the concession.

Claimants:
 Original: **Chapard, Nicholas**
 Present: **William M'Intosh**
 50 acres, not surveyed.

Claimants:
 Original: **Cartier, Pierre**
 Present: **Henry Vanderburgh**
 92.80 acres, surveyed; on Mill creek, joining -- **McGowen** and other lands of -- **Vanderburgh**.

Claimants:
 Original: **Cartier, Pierre**
 Present: **Francis Vigo**
 43.80 acres, surveyed; on Mill creek, joining -- **McGowen** and other lands of -- **Vanderburgh**.

Claimants:
 Original: **Cartier, Pierre**
 Present: **James Ledgerwood**
 264 acres, surveyed; on Bosseron creek.

Claimants:
 Original: **Connoyer, Pierre**
 Present: **Pierre Connoyer**, heirs of
 68 acres, surveyed; in the upper prairie, joining **H. Vanderburgh** and **F. Vigo**.

Claimants:
 Original: **Connoyer, Pierre**
 Present: **Pierre Connoyer**, heirs of
 50 acres, not surveyed.

Claimants:
 Original: **Chabert, Jean**
 Present: **Alexander Valli**
 50 acres, surveyed; on northwest side of Wabash, at ther Nutt river, joining said Valli.

Claimants:
 Original: **Charbonneau, Jacques**
 Present: **Robert Buntin**
 100 acres, surveyed; on southeast side of Wabash, joining lands late of **Jacques Lacroix**, now Buntin's, and lands late of **J. Baird**.

Claimants:

Original: **Cardinal, Jacques**
Present: **Robert Buntin**
100 acres, surveyed; on the east, and joining the donation and lands late of J. Cardinal, now Buntin's.

Claimants:
Original: **Chapard, Nicholas**
Present: **Robert Buntin**
408.50 acres, surveyed; on Mill creek, joining other lands of R. Buntin and **H. Vanderburgh**.

Claimants:
Original: **Chartier, Joseph**
Present: **Robert Buntin**
34.80 acres, surveyed; in the upper prairie, joining other lands of R. Buntin and **F. Vigo**.

Claimants:
Original: **Charbonneau, Jacques**
Present: **Francis Vigo**
68.24 acres, surveyed; in upper prairie, joining widow of **A. Lefevre**.

Claimants:
Original: **Chartier, Joseph**
Present: **Francis Vigo**
34.80 acres; surveyed; in upper prairie, joining lands of **James Charbonneau**.

Claimants:
Original: **Cardinal, Nicholas**
Present: **Francis Vigo**
68.24 acres, surveyed; in upper prairie, joining lands late of **A. Guarguipie**.

Claimants:
Original: **Coder, Rene**
Present: **Francis Vigo**
272 acres, surveyed; on Mill creek, joining -- **Simpson**, -- **McClure**, and **J. R. Jones**.

Claimants:
Original: **Chartier, Jean Baptiste**
Present: **Francis Vigo**
68.16 acres, not surveyed; granted, on northwest side of Wabash, opposite Vincennes.

Claimants:
 Original: **Clark, George R.**
 Present: **William Clark**
 272 acres, not surveyed; granted, at the Little village.

Claimants:
 Original: **Cuntz, Felix**
 Present: **John R. Jones**
 165.40 acres, surveyed; on River Des Chis, bounded by **Minard Asturgas, J. Minor,** and **J. R. Jones.**

Claimants:
 Original: **Cuntz, Felix**
 Present: **Jacob Minor**
 175 acres, surveyed; on River Des Chis, bounded by **J. R. Jones, George Catt,** and vacant lands.

Claimants:
 Original: **Coder, Francis,** heirs of
 Present: **Christopher Wyant**
 50 acres, not surveyed.

Claimants:
 Original: **Coulen, Jacques, alias Chataway**
 Present: **John Small**
 340.40 acres, surveyed; at the Black Ground, on Embarrass [river].

Claimants:
 Original: **Chabotte, Joseph**
 Present: **Andre Racine Ste. Marie**
 50 acres, not surveyed.

Claimants:
 Original: **Cardine, Jean**
 Present: **Peter Barrackman,** heirs of
 340.28 acres, surveyed; on river Des Chis, Barrackman's station.

Claimants:
 Original: **Cardine, Jean**
 Present: **Peter Barrackman,** heirs of
 144.60 acres, surveyed; on river Des Chis, Barrackman's station.

Claimants:
 Original: **Cardine, Louis**
 Present: **Peter Barrackman,** heirs of
 195.140 acres, not surveyed.

Claimants:
Original: **Cardine, Jean**
Present: **George Fidler**
136.16 acres, surveyed; on north of White river, joining said Fidler and others.

Claimants:
Original: **Coder, Pierre**, heirs of
Present: **Pierre Corder**, heirs of
50 acres, not surveyed.

Claimants:
Original: **Divore, Philip**
Present: **Philip Divore**
300 acres, surveyed; on river Des Chis, bounded by -- **Reed, John Pea, Seb[astian?] Frederick**, and others.

Claimants:
Original: **Dagenet, Francois**
Present: **John Crawford**, heirs of
50 acres, not surveyed.

Claimants:
Original: **Decker, Tobias**
Present: **Adam Harness**
85 acres, surveyed; on White river, bounded by donations and by **Isaac Decker**.

Claimants:
Original: **Decker, Moses, Senior**
Present: **Moses Decker**
300 acres, surveyed; on waters of river Des Chis, bounded by **B. Beckes, John Pea, T. Jordon***, and others. [*so spelled]

Claimants:
Original: **Delaurier, Jean Baptiste**
Present: **Jean Baptiste Delaurier**
136.16 acres, surveyed; in Cathelinette prairie.

Claimants:
Original: **Derozier, --, alias Pipi Bonaventure**
Present: **Benjamin D. Price**
136 acres, surveyed; on Marie creek, joining other lands of said Price.

Claimants:
Original: **Dizi, Barbara**
Present: **Benjamin D. Price**
50 acres, surveyed; on Marie creek.

Claimants:
 Original: **Decker, John**
 Present: **Abraham Decker, Senior**
160 acres, surveyed; on river Des Chis, joining **B. Beckes, Moses Decker, John Pea,** and **P. Catt.**

Claimants:
 Original: **Decker, John**
 Present: **Abraham Decker, Senior**
134 acres, surveyed; on south side of White river, joining **Joseph Decker,** and heirs of **John Glass.**

Claimants:
 Original: **Decker, John**
 Present: **Abraham Decker, Senior**
50 acres, surveyed; on waters of river Des Chis, joining **B. Beckes** and **J. Pea.**

Claimants:
 Original: **Duchesne, Jean Baptiste**
 Present: **Antoine Marchal**
65.16 acres, surveyed; on waters of Mill creek.

Claimants:
 Original: **Duchesne, Jean Baptiste**
 Present: **Jean Baptiste Duchesne,** heirs of
62.32 acres, surveyed; on waters of Mill creek.

Claimants:
 Original: **Duchesne, Jean Baptiste**
 Present: **Abraham Kuykindall**
50 acres, surveyed; on White river, joining other lands of said Kuykindall.

Claimants:
 Original: **Denoyon, -- (Jean Baptiste?)**
 Present: **James Johnston, Esq.**
306.32 acres, surveyed; on waters of Mill creek, joining the donation, **J. R. Jones,** and others.

Claimants:
 Original: **Denoyon, Louis,** widow of
 Present: **Ursule** and **Julie Bosseron**
200 acres, surveyed; on northwest side Wabash, joining -- **Dubois** and -- **Marchal.**

Claimants:
 Original: **Denoyon, Louis**, widow of
 Present: **William H. Harrison**
200 acres, surveyed; on northwest side Wabash, joining -- **Dubois** and -- **Marchal**.

Claimants:
 Original: **Drouet, alias Richardville, Antoine**
 Present: **Ursule** and **Julie Bosseron**
50 acres, surveyed; on northwest side Wabash, joining said **Julie** and **Ursule [Bosseron]**.

[ASP 8:1:562]

Claimants:
 Original: **Dudevoir, alias Lachine, Charles**
 Present: **William H. Harrison**
68.24 acres, surveyed; in the upper prairie, joining **F. Vigo**.

Claimants:
 Original: **Danis*, Antoine**
 Present: **William Morrison** and heirs of **A. Danis**.
68.16 acres, surveyed; granted in the lower prairie, joining **P. Bono** and **A. Marie**. [*so spelled]

Claimants:
 Original: **Denis*, Jacques**
 Present: **Toussaint Dubois**
102.12 acres, surveyed; on Embarras river, joining other lands of said Dubois. [*so spelled]

Claimants:
 Original: **Dalton, Valentine**
 Present: **Toussaint Dubois**
136.16 acres, surveyed; on Embarrass river, joining **Jacques Denis** and others.

Claimants:
 Original: **Dubois, Toussaint**
 Present: **Jean Baptiste Dubois**, heirs of
68.24 acres, surveyed; in the lower prairie, joining heirs of **F. Hamtramck** and -- **Roy**.

Claimants:
 Original: **Dubois, Jean Baptiste**
 Present: **Jean Baptiste Dubois**, heirs of
 50 acres, not surveyed.

Claimants:
 Original: **Decouteaux, Joseph**
 Present: **Luke Decker, Esq.**
 68.16 acres, surveyed; on river Des Chis, joining said Decker.

Claimants:
 Original: **Decker, Luke**
 Present: **Luke Decker, Esq.**
 340.44 acres, surveyed; on river Des Chis, joining said Decker.

Claimants:
 Original: **Decker, Joseph, Senior**
 Present: **Abraham Decker**
 300 acres, surveyed; on southeast side of White river, adjoining **Isaac Decker**.

Claimants:
 Original: **Decker, Isaac**
 Present: **Isaac Decker**, heirs of
 340.44 acres, surveyed; on north side White river, joining **Adam Harness** and others.

Claimants:
 Original: **Drouet, alias Richardville, Antoine**
 Present: **Antoine Drouet**
 17 acres, not surveyed.

Claimants:
 Original: **Dugal, Antoine**
 Present: **Thomas Jones**
 50 acres, not surveyed.

Claimants:
 Original: **Dagneau, --**
 Present: **Henry Vanderburgh**
 68.16 acres, surveyed; in the upper prairie, joining **P. Bonneau** and **J. Dorret**.

Claimants:
 Original: **Delisle, Charles**
 Present: **Isaac, Minor**
 50 acres, surveyed; on waters of White river, joining **W. Mays**.

Claimants:
 Original: **Ditard, Jean**
 Present: **Samuel Baird**
 34 acres, not surveyed; on northwest side of Wabash, joining **Pierre Cornoye** and **J. Brassard**.

Claimants:
 Original: **Ducharme, Joseph**
 Present: **J. F. Hamtramck**, heirs of
 136.16 acres; surveyed; on northwest side of Wabash, joining -- **Bazadone's** and -- **Hunot**.

Claimants:
 Original: **Dubois, Jean Baptiste**
 Present: **Francis Vigo**
 136.16 acres, surveyed; in the barrens at Belle Fontaine. Survey not returned.

Claimants:
 Original: **Dubois, Jean Baptiste**
 Present: **Francis Vigo**
 68.16 acres, surveyed; in the barrens at Belle Fontaine. Survey not returned.

Claimants:
 Original: **Dalton, Valentine T.**
 Present: **John R. Jones**
 340.44 acres, surveyed; on the river Des Chis, joining land late of **F. Kintz**.

Claimants:
 Original: **Danis, Antoine**
 Present: **William Morrison**
 34 acres, not surveyed; granted joining the common fence in the white oak level.

Claimants:
 Original: **Danis, Antoine**
 Present: Not entered
 102 acres, not surveyed.

Claimants:
 Original: **Denoyon, Louis**
 Present: Not entered
 68.16 acres, surveyed; in the lower prairie, joining -- **Edline** and **Francis Mallet**.

Claimants:
 Original: **Dudevore, Charles, alias Lachine**
 Present: **Charles Dudevore**
 68.16 acres, surveyed; in the lower prairie, joining **Michel Bordeleau** and **Francis Mallett**.

Claimants:
 Original: **Dizi, --**
 Present: **William McIntosh**
 340.44 acres, not surveyed.

Claimants:
 Original: **Decker, Abraham**
 Present: **Abraham Decker**
 200 acres, not surveyed.

Claimants:
 Original: **Dube, --**
 Present: **John R. Jones**
 136.16 acres, not surveyed.

Claimants:
 Original: **Dalton, Hannah**
 Present: **Henry Cassady**
 136.16 acres, not surveyed; granted on northwest side Wabash, bounded by **T. Dubois** and others.

Claimants:
 Original: **Edline, Alexis, Joseph, and Nicholas**
 Present: **Thomas Baird**
 200 acres, surveyed; on waters of Wabash, joining **R. Bantin**, heirs of **F. Hambramck** and others.

Claimants:
 Original: **Edline, Louis**
 Present: **John Durham**
 50 acres, surveyed; on Marie creek, joining said Durham's mill tract.

Claimants:
 Original: **Edline, Alexis, Joseph, and Nicholas**
 Present: **Dubois, Toussaint**
 200 acres, surveyed; on Wabash, at the Little Rock, joining heirs of **N. Perrot**, **T. Baird**, and **R. Buntin**.

Claimants:
 Original: **Edline, Louis**
 Present: **Vincent Lafoy**
 68.16 acres, surveyed; in lower prairie, joining the church lands.

Claimants:
 Original: **Edline, Louis**
 Present: **Louis Edline**, heirs of **William Bullett**
 68.16 acres, surveyed; in lower prairie, joining **V. Lafoy** and **F. Vigo**.

Claimants:
 Original: **Edline, Louis**
 Present: **Andre des Biens**
 57 acres, surveyed; in lower prairie, joining lands late of **L. Edline** and **F. Vigo**.

Claimants:
 Original: **Edline, Louis**
 Present: **Louis Edline**, heirs of
 56.100 acres, surveyed; in lower prairie, joining **A. Caty** and **F. Vigo**.

Claimants:
 Original: **Frederick, Lewis**
 Present: **Lewis Frederick**
 66 acres, surveyed; on the Muddy run, bounded by **William Reed**, **P. Devore**, and said Frederick.

Claimants:
 Original: **Frederick, Lewis**
 Present: **Lewis Frederick**
 234 acres, surveyed; on Conger's creek, on southeast side of White river.

Claimants:
 Original: **Frederick, Sebastian**
 Present: **Sebastian Frederick**, heirs of
 300 acres, surveyed; on White river bounded by **P. Catt**.

Claimants:
 Original: **Frederick, Peter**
 Present: **Peter Frederick**
 300 acres, surveyed; on waters of White river, bounded by **J. Mayo**.

Claimants:
 Original: **Frederick, Sebastian**
 Present: **Sebastian Frederick**
 300 acres, surveyed; on waters of Whited river, bounded by the heirs of -- **Glass** and **M. Thorn**.

Claimants:
 Original: **Foyzis, Francois**
 Present: **Antoine Marchal**
 50 acres, not surveyed.

Claimants:
 Original: **Fernsley, William**
 Present: **William Fernsley**
 255 acres, not surveyed.

Claimants:
 Original: **Fernsley, William**
 Present: **William Fernsley**
 400 acres, not surveyed.

Claimants:
 Original: **Goder, Louis**
 Present: not entered
 34 acres, surveyed; in the Cathelinette prairie, joining heirs of **Jos[eph] Lafeuillade** and -- **Delaurier**.

Claimants:
 Original: **Goder, Louis**
 Present: **Louis Goder,** heirs of
 34 acres, surveyed; in the Cathelinette prairie.

Claimants:
 Original: **Glass, John**
 Present: **John Glass,** heirs of
 300 acres, surveyed; on east side White river, bounded by **S. Frederick, J. Decker**, and heirs of -- **Bosseron**.

Claimants:
 Original: **Gamelin, Pierre**
 Present: **Henry Kirk**
 50 acres,m surveyed; on Potoka, joining the No. 104 and 105 of the militia lands.

[ASP 8:1:563]

Claimants:
 Original: **Gamelin, Paul**
 Present: **Paul Gamelin,** heirs of
34 acres, surveyed; north side of the Wabash, bounded by **R. Buntin, P. Cornoye,** and the Wabash.

Claimants:
 Original: **Gamelin, Pierre, Senior & Junior**
 Present: **Antoine Marchal**
272.32 acres, surveyed; at the Little Rock on the Wabash.

Claimants:
 Original: **Gamelin, Paul**
 Present: **Antoine Marchal**
4 acres, not surveyed; in the Indian fields.

Claimants:
 Original: **Grimmare, Pierre**
 Present: **George Catt**
68.16 acres, not surveyed; granted on river Des Chis, joining **Jacob Minor,** and other lands of said Catt.

Claimants:
 Original: **Gamelin, Pierre**
 Present: **William McIntosh**
340.44 acres, surveyed; at the grand rapids on the west side of Wabash.

Claimants:
 Original: **Gamelin, Paul**
 Present: **William McIntosh**
136.16 acres, surveyed; at the Little Rock, above Vincennes, joining **D. Smith,** and others.

Claimants:
 Original: **Guarguipie, Amable**
 Present: **Francis Vigo**
68.16 acres, surveyed; in the upper prairie, joining lands late of **G. Chartier** and **N. Cardinal.**

Claimants:
 Original: **Gamelin, Paul**
 Present: **Francis Vigo**
34.8 acres, surveyed; in the upper prairie.

Claimants:
 Original: **Grimarre, Pierre,** heirs of
 Present: **Toussaint Dubois**
 50 acres, not surveyed.

Claimants:
 Original: **Gamelin, Pierre**
 Present: **Andre Racine Ste. Marie**
 68.16 acres, surveyed; in Cathelinette prairie, joining --
 Barrois, and heirs of **A. Peltier.**

Claimants:
 Original: **Guilbea, Charles**
 Present: **John R. Jones**
 136.16 acres, not surveyed.

Claimants:
 Original: **Goder, Louis**
 Present: not entered
 50 acres; not surveyed.

Claimants:
 Original: **Holliday, James**
 Present: **Joseph Millburn**
 200 acres, surveyed; on southeast side of White river and Potoka creek, joining **William Mills.**

Claimants:
 Original: **Harbin, Joshua**
 Present: **Joshua Harbin,** heirs of
 300 acres, not surveyed.

Claimants:
 Original: **Harbin, John**
 Present: **John Marshal**
 300 acres, surveyed; on Conger's creek, southeast side of White river, joining **George Leech.**

Claimants:
 Original: **Hall, Christian**
 Present: **Philip Catt**
 50 acres, surveyed; on south side of White river, joining **John Marshal,** and bottom of White river.

Claimants:
 Original: **Hall, Christian**
 Present: **Philip Catt**
 300 acres, not surveyed.

Claimants:
 Original: **Hall, William**
 Present: **Toussaint Dubois**
 136.16 acres, surveyed; on Embarras river, joining other land of said Dubois.

Claimants:
 Original: **Hinton, Vatchel**
 Present: **Jeremiah Claypole**
 225 acres, not surveyed.

Claimants:
 Original: **Vatchel Hinton**
 Present: **Vatchel Hinton**, heirs of
 75 acres, not surveyed.

Claimants:
 Original: **Hall, Thomas**
 Present: **Toussaint, Dubois**
 136.16 acres, surveyed; on Embarrass river, joining other lands of said Dubois.

Claimants:
 Original: **Harpin, Jean Baptiste**
 Present: **Luke Decker, Esq.**
 136.16 acres, surveyed; on river Des Chis, joining **John Small**.

Claimants:
 Original: **Hunot, Joseph**
 Present: **Hugh Heward***
 136.16 acres, surveyed; on the west side of the Wabash, joining **J. F. Hamtramck** and -- **Vigo**.

Claimants:
 Original: **Hunot, Gabriel**
 Present: **Christopher Wyant**
 50 acres, not surveyed.

Claimants:
 Original: **Howell, Jacob**, heirs of
 Present: **Christopher Wyant**
 200 acres, not surveyed.

Claimants:
 Original: **Howell, Jacob**, heirs of
 Present: **John R. Jones**
 340.44 acres; surveyed; two hundred acres specified, joining **B. D. Price** on south; **D. Price** on east, the remainder of this tract taken up by other claims.

Claimants:
 Original: **Henry, Moses**
 Present: **Luke Decker, Esq.**
 136.16 acres, not surveyed.

Claimants:
 Original: **Hamelin, Joseph**
 Present: **George Fidler**
 136.16 acres, surveyed; no north side White river, joining said **Fuller**, and others.

Claimants:
 Original: **Hall, William**
 Present: **William Hall**
 136.16 acres, not surveyed.

Claimants:
 Original: **Henry, Moses**
 Present: **Abraham F. Snapp**
 136.16 acres, not surveyed; at the little village on north side Wabash.

Claimants:
 Original: **Harpin, Jean Baptiste**
 Present: **Jean Baptiste Harpin**
 68.16 acres, surveyed; in the lower prairie, joining **F. Languedoc**, and others.

Claimants:
 Original: **Harpin, Jean Baptiste**
 Present: **Jean Baptiste Harpin**
 68.16 acres, surveyed; in the lower prairie.

Claimants:
 Original: **Johnson, Richard**
 Present: **Jacob Minor**
 150 acres, surveyed; on waters of river Des Chis, bounded by **Luke Decker**.

Claimants:
 Original: **Johnson, James** (turner)
 Present: **James Johnson**
 300 acres, surveyed; on the waters of White river, bounded by **B. Reed, T. Jordan**, and **F. Biddle**.

Claimants:
 Original: **Jennings, Robert**
 Present: **William Morrison**, heirs of
 136.16 acres, not surveyed.

Claimants:
 Original: **Johnson, James, Esq.**
 Present: **James Johnson, Esq.**
 400 acres, not surveyed.

Claimants:
 Original: **Johnson, James, Esq.**
 Present: **James Johnson, Esq.**
 300 acres, surveyed; on Bosseron creek, joining.

Claimants:
 Original: **Johnson, Robert**
 Present: **John R. Jones**
 229 acres, surveyed; on waters of river Des Chis, joining **B. Beckes, M. Asturgas, G. Leech,** and others.

Claimants:
 Original: **Johnson, Robert**
 Present: **Samuel Applegate**
 50 acres, surveyed.

Claimants:
 Original: **Langlois, Rene**
 Present: **Gabriel Hunot**
 68.16 acres, surveyed; in Cathelinette prairie, joining -- **Barrois** and -- **Bordeleau.**

Claimants:
 Original: **Lognon, Francois**
 Present: not entered
 50 acres, surveyed; on waters of river Des Chis, joining **F. Mehl** and the lines of the commons.

Claimants:
 Original: **Laderoute, Alexis**
 Present: **Laurent Bazadone**
 136.16 acres, not surveyed; granted at the little village.

Claimants:
 Original: **Laderoute, Alexis**
 Present: not entered
 34 acres, not surveyed; granted at the little village.

Claimants:
 Original: **Levine, Joseph**
 Present: **Joseph Levine,** heirs of
 200 acres, surveyed; on the southeast side of the Wabash, joining **Jacob Plough.**

Claimants:
 Original: **Legrand, Jean M.**
 Present: **Thomas Jordon***
 120 acres, surveyed; on waters of White river, bounded by **James Johnson** and **M. Decker**. [*so spelled]

Claimants:
 Original: **Legrand, Jean M.**
 Present: **Jeremiah Claypole**
 230 acres, not surveyed.

Claimants:
 Original: **Lefevre, alias Chapeau, Antoine**
 Present: **Thomas Jones**
 68.16 acres, not surveyed.

Claimants:
 Original: **Levine, Richard**
 Present: **Benjamin D. Price**
 300 acres, surveyed; on waters of Marie creek.

Claimants:
 Original: **Latrimouille, Jacques**
 Present: **Benjamin D. Price**
 108.128 acres, surveyed; on waters of Marie creek, joining other lands of B. D. Price.

Claimants:
 Original: **Latrimouille, Jacques**
 Present: not entered
 27.032 acres, surveyed; on waters of Marie creek, joining the above.

Claimants:
 Original: **Languedoc, Francois**
 Present: **Luke Decker, Junior**
 50 acres, surveyed; on southeast side of White river, joining **J. Decker**.

SURNAME INDEX

Adam, Harness, 12
Addison, William, 11
Applegate, Samuel, 37
Ardrine, L., 11
Arpin, Jean Baptiste, 11
Aschar, Joseph, 11
Askin, John, 12
Askins, John, 14
Astrus, Alexis, dit Guiguvlet, 11
Asturgas, Minor, 11
Asturgas, Minor, heirs of, 11
Asturgas, Minor, 11
Asturgas, Minor, heirs of, 11
Asturgas, Minard, 12
Asturgas, Minard, 24
Asturgas, M., 37
Badollet, John, 10
Baillorjon, Nicholas, 17
Baillorjon, Nicholas, heirs of, 17
Baily, John, 15
Baird, S., 19
Baird, J., 22
Baird, Samuel, 29
Baird, Thomas, 30
Baird, T., 30
Bantin, Robert, 19
Bantin, R., 30
Bantin. See also Buntin, 19
Barrackman, Henry, 13
Barrackman, Peter, 14
Barrackman, Peter, heirs of, 14
Barrackman, Peter, heirs of, 16
Barrackman, Peter, heirs of, 16
Barrackman, Christopher, 19
Barrackman, Christopher, heirs of, 19
Barrackman, Abraham, 19
Barrackman, Peter, heirs of, 24
Barrackman, Peter, heirs of, 24
Barren, Joseph, 02
Barril, Francois, 12
Barrois, --, 34
Barrois, --, 37
Barthe, Pierre, 18
Bazadone, Laurent, 12
Bazadone, --, 29
Bazadone, Laurent, 37

Bazinette, Francois, 16
Beauchain, Jean Baptiste, 07
Beauchain, Jean Baptiste, 16
Beauchain. See Jean Baptiste Racine
Beauchene, Jean Baptiste, 08
Beauchene, Jean Baptiste, heirs of, 10
Beauchene. S. Jean Baptiste Racine, 07
Beckes, Benjamin, 11
Beckes, Benjamin, 12
Beckes, Benjamin, 13
Beckes, Benjamin, 13
Beckes, Benjamin, 13
Beckes, Benjamin, 20
Beckes, B., 25
Beckes, B., 26
Beckes, B., 26
Beckes, B., 37
Beedle, Elias, 14
Bergand, Charles, 16
Bergand, Dominique, 17
Bergand, Dominique, 21
Berger, Frederick, 11
Berger, Frederick, 12
Berger, Peter, 13
Berger, Peter, 13
Berger, Frederick, Junior, 14
Berger, Frederick, heirs of, 14
Berger, --, 14
Berger, Frederick, Senior, 15
Berger, George, 18
Berger, George, 18
Berger, George, heirs of, 18
Bergeron, Louis, 16
Bergeron, Louis, 18
Biddle, F., 36
Biens, Andre des. See des Biens
Binette, Jean Baptiste, 14
Binette, Jean Baptiste, 14
Binette, Jean Baptiste, 18
Black, --, 14
Black, --, 15
Bolon, Hypolite, 13
Bolon, Amable, 14
Bolon, Louis, 15
Bonaventure. See Derozier
Bondy, Antoine, 12
Bonhomme, Jean Baptiste, 13
Bonneau, Charles, Senior, 19
Bonneau, P., 28

Bono, Nicholas, 17
Bono, P., 27
Bordeleau, Antoine, 12
Bordeleau, Antoine, 15
Bordeleau, Antoine, heirs of, 12
Bordeleau, Michel, heirs, 14
Bordeleau, Jean Baptiste, 19
Bordeleau, M., 19
Bordeleau, Michel, 30
Bordeleau, --, 37
Borneau, Charles, 17
Bosseron, Francois, 02
Bosseron, --, 02
Bosseron, --, 17
Bosseron, --, 32
Bosseron, Francois, 02
Bosseron, Francois, 02
Bosseron, Francois, 12
Bosseron, Francois, 14
Bosseron, Francois, 15
Bosseron, Francois, 15
Bosseron, Francois, 16
Bosseron, Francois, 17
Bosseron, Francois, 18
Bosseron, Francois, 18
Bosseron, Jean Baptiste, 19
Bosseron, Julie, 26
Bosseron, Julie, 27
Bosseron, Ursule, 27
Bosseron, Ursule, 27
Boucher, Vital, 14
Boucher, Vital, 15
Boucher, Vital, and her heirs, 19
Boyer, Francois, 12
Boyer, Francois, 15
Boyer, Louis, 17
Boyer, Louis, 18
Boyer, Peter, 17
Boyer, Toussaint, 16
Brassard, J., 29
Brouillette, M., 14
Brouillette, Michel, 18
Bullett, Benjamin, 19
Bullett, William, 11
Bullett, William, heirs of, 31
Buntin, Robert, 02
Buntin, Robert, Esq., 08
Buntin, R., 16
Buntin, Robert, 18

Buntin, Robert, 18
Buntin, Robert, 22
Buntin, Robert, 23
Buntin, Robert, 23
Buntin, Robert, 23
Buntin, R., 30
Buntin, R., 33
Buntin. See also Bantin, 19
Byerjeon, Nicholas, 19
Cabassier, Pierre, 09
Cardide, Jean, 21
Cardinal, Nicholas, heirs of, 02
Cardinal, Jean Baptiste, 19
Cardinal, Jacques, 20
Cardinal, Jacques, 23
Cardinal, Nicholas, 23
Cardinal, N., 33
Cardine, Jean, 24
Cardine, Jean, 25
Cardine, Louis, 24
Carmichael, James, 20
Carter, Moses, 13
Carter, Moses, 20
Cartier, Pierre, 05
Cartier, Pierre, 22
Cartier, Pierre, 22
Cartier, Pierre, 22
Cassady, Henry, 30
Catt, George, 24
Catt, George, 31
Catt, P., 11
Catt, P., 26
Catt, P., 31
Catt, Philip, 21
Catt, Philip, 34
Catt, Philip, 34
Caty, Antoine, 20
Caty, Antoine, heirs of, 20
Caty, A., 31
Chabert, --, widow of, 19
Chabert, Jean, 22
Chabotte, Joseph, 24
Chapard, Nicholas, 02
Chapard, N., 17
Chapard, Nicholas, Junior, 21
Chapard, Nicholas, Junior, heirs of, 21
Chapard, Nicholas, 22
Chapard, Nicholas, 23
Chapart, Nicholas, 21

Chapart, Nicholas, heirs of, 21
Chapart, Nicholas, 21
Chapart, Nicholas, heirs of, 21
Chapeau. See Antoine Lefevre
Charbonneau, Jacques, 20
Charbonneau, Jacques, 22
Charbonneau, Jacques, 23
Charbonneau, James, 23
Chartier Debeauch, Joseph, 21
Chartier, G., 33
Chartier, J. B., 18
Chartier, Jean Baptiste, 23
Chartier, Joseph, 20
Chartier, Joseph, 23
Chartier, Joseph, 23
Chataway. See Jacques Coulen
Clark, George R., 24
Clark, William, 24
Claypole, Jeremiah, 15
Claypole, Jeremiah, 15
Claypole, Jeremiah, 35
Claypole, Jeremiah, 38
Coder, Pierre, widow of, 19
Coder, Andre, 21
Coder, Francois, 21
Coder, Francis, 21
Coder, Francis, heirs of, 24
Coder, Pierre, heirs of, 25
Coder, Rene, 23
Coder, Rene, Junior, 20
Connoyer, Pierre, 22
Connoyer, Pierre, heirs of, 22
Connoyer, Pierre, 22
Connoyer, Pierre, heirs of, 22
Cornoye, Pierre, 29
Cornoye, P., 33
Cornoyer, [Angelique; nee Racine], 06
Cornoyer, Angelique [nee Racine], 07
Coulen, Jacques, dit Chataway, 24
Crawford, John, heirs of, 25
Crock, David, 13
Cuntz, Felix, 24
Cuntz, Felix, 24
Cuntz. See also Kintz
Dagenet, Ambrose, 02
Dagenet, Ambrose, 02
Dagenet, Ambrose, 02
Dagenet, Francois, 25
Dagneau, --, 14

Dagneau, --, 14
Dagneau, --, 28
Dalton, Valentine, 27
Dalton, Valentine T., 29
Dalton, Hannah, 30
Danis, A., heirs of, 27
Danis, Antoine, 27
Danis, Antoine, 29
Danis, Antoine, 29
Debeauch. See Chartier Debeauch
Decker, Abraham, Senior, 25
Decker, Abraham, Senior, 26
Decker, Abraham, 28
Decker, Abraham, 30
Decker, Isaac, heirs of, 1
Decker, Isaac, heirs of, 28
Decker, Isaac, 03
Decker, Isaac, 25
Decker, Isaac, 28
Decker, Isaac, 28
Decker, J., 18
Decker, J., 18
Decker, J., 32
Decker, J., 38
Decker, John, 26
Decker, John, 26
Decker, John, 26
Decker, John, 26
Decker, Joseph, 26
Decker, Joseph, Senior, 28
Decker, Luke, Esq., 28
Decker, Luke, 13
Decker, Luke, 28
Decker, Luke, Esq., 28
Decker, Luke, Esq., 35
Decker, Luke, Esq., 36
Decker, Luke, 36
Decker, Luke, Junior, 38
Decker, M., 38
Decker, Moses, 25
Decker, Moses, 26
Decker, Tobias, 25
Decointre, --, heirs of, 14
Decotteaux, --, 05
Decouteaux, Joseph, 28
Delaurier, Jean Baptiste, 25
Delaurier, --, 32
Delisle, Charles, 28
Denis, Jacques, 27

Denis, Jacques, 27
Denoyon, Angelique [nee Racine], 06
Denoyon, Angelique [nee Racine], 07
Denoyon, --, 26
Denoyon, Jean Baptiste, 26
Denoyon, L., 04
Denoyon, Louis, widow of, 26
Denoyon, Louis, widow of, 27
Denoyon, Louis, 29
Derousse, P., 14
Derousse, P., 14
Derozier, --, dit Pipi Bonaventure, 25
Des Biens, Andre, 31
Devore, P., 31
Ditard, Jean, 29
Divore, Philip, 25
Dizi, Barbara, 25
Dizi, --, 30
Dorret, J., 28
Drouet, Antoine, did Richardville, 27
Drouet, Antoine, dit Richardville, 28
Dube, --, 30
Dubois, --, 14
Dubois, --, 26
Dubois, --, 27
Dubois, Jean Baptiste, heirs of, 27
Dubois, Jean Baptiste, 28
Dubois, Jean Baptiste, heirs of, 28
Dubois, Jean Baptiste, 29
Dubois, Jean Baptiste, 29
Dubois, T., 30
Dubois, Toussaint, 15
Dubois, Toussaint, 16
Dubois, Toussaint, 16
Dubois, Toussaint, 16
Dubois, Toussaint, 16
Dubois, Toussaint, 27
Dubois, Toussaint, 27
Dubois, Toussaint, 27
Dubois, Toussaint, 30
Dubois, Toussaint, 34
Dubois, Toussaint, 35
Dubois, Toussaint, 35
Ducharme, Joseph, 29
DuChesne, Jean Baptiste, heirs of, 02
Duchesne, Jean Baptiste, heirs of, 26
Duchesne, Jean Baptiste, 26
Duchesne, Jean Baptiste, 26
Duchesne, Jean Baptiste, 26

Dudevoir, Charles, dit Lachine, 27
Dudevore, Charles, dit Lachine, 30
Dugal, Antoine, 28
Durham, John, 30
Edline, --, 29
Edline, Alexis, 30
Edline, Alexis, 30
Edline, Joseph, 30
Edline, Joseph, 30
Edline, Joseph, 30
Edline, L., 31
Edline, Louis, 31
Edline, Louis, 31
Edline, Louis, 31
Edline, Louis, heirs of, 31
Edline, Nicholas, 30
Edline, Nicholas, 30
Ewing, Nathaniel, Esq., 10
Fernsley, William, 32
Fernsley, William, 32
Fidler, George, 25
Fidler, George, 36
Flower, Thomas, 02
Flower, Thomas, 02
Flower, Thomas, 03
Flower, Thomas, 03
Flower, Thomas, 03
Flower, Thomas, 03
Flower, Thomas, 03
Fortin, Louis N., 11
Foyzis, Francois, 32
Frederick, Peter, 11
Frederick, S., 21
Frederick, L., 21
Frederick, Sebastian, 25
Frederick, Lewis, 31
Frederick, Lewis, 31
Frederick, Peter, 31
Frederick, Sebastian, 25
Frederick, Sebastian, 31
Frederick, Sebastian, heirs of, 31
Frederick, Sebastian, 32
Frederick, S., 32
Gallatin, Albert, Esq., 10
Gamelin, P., 18
Gamelin, Paul, 33
Gamelin, Paul, 33
Gamelin, Paul, 33
Gamelin, Paul, heirs of, 02

Gamelin, Paul, heirs of, 33
Gamelin, Pierre, 02
Gamelin, Pierre, 03
Gamelin, Pierre, 03
Gamelin, Pierre, 03
Gamelin, Pierre, 03
Gamelin, Pierre, 03
Gamelin, Pierre, 03
Gamelin, Pierre, 32
Gamelin, Pierre, Senior, 33
Gamelin, Pierre, Junior, 33
Gamelin, Pierre, 33
Gamelin, Pierre, 34
Gibson, John, 04
Gibson, John, 04
Gibson, John, 04
Gibson, John, Secretary Indiana Territory, 07
Gibson, --, General, 07
Gibson, --, General, 21
Glass, --, heirs of, 32
Glass, John, 16
Glass, John, 26
Glass, John, 32
Glass, John, heirs of, 32
Goder, Louis, 32
Goder, Louis, 32
Goder, Louis, heirs of, 32
Goder, Louis, 34
Goder, P., 17
Gonzalis, Simon, 18
Grimarre, Pierre, heirs of, 34
Grimmare, Pierre, 33
Guarguipie, A., 23
Guarguipie, Amable, 33
Guiguvlet. See Alexis Astrus
Guilbea, Charles, 34
Hall, Christian, 34
Hall, Christian, 34
Hall, Thomas, 25
Hall, William, 35
Hall, William, 36
Hamelin, Joseph, 08
Hamelin, Joseph, 08
Hamelin, Joseph, 08
Hamelin, Joseph, 08
Hamelin, Joseph, 08
Hamelin, Joseph, 09
Hamelin, Francois, 09
Hamelin, Joseph, 36

Hamtramck, F., 30
Hamtramck, F., heirs of, 27
Hamtramck, Jean F., heirs of, 17
Hamtramck, J. F., heirs of, 29
Hamtramck, J. F., 35
Harbin, John, 07
Harbin, John, 34
Harbin, Joshua, heirs of, 19
Harbin, Joshua, 34
Harbin, Joshua, heirs of, 34
Harness, --, 13
Harness, Adam, 19
Harness, Adam, 25
Harness, Adam, 28
Harpin, Jean Baptiste, 35
Harpin, Jean Baptiste, 36
Harpin, Jean Baptiste, 36
Harrison, William, 02
Harrison, [William], Governor, 09
Harrison, William H., 15
Harrison, William H., 15
Harrison, William H., 15
Harrison, William H., 21
Harrison, William H., 27
Harrison, William H., 27
Henry, Moses, 36
Henry, Moses, 36
Heward, Hugh, 35
Hinton, Vatchel, 35
Hinton, Vatchel, 35
Hinton, Vatchel, heirs of, 35
Holder, Thomas, 20
Holliday, James, 34
Howard. See Heward
Howell, Jacob, heirs of, 35
Howell, Jacob, heirs of, 35
Hunot, --, 29
Hunot, Gabriel, 35
Hunot, Gabriel, 37
Hunot, Joseph, 35
Hunt, Henry, clerk of the territorial general court, 10
Jennings, Robert, 36
Johnson, R., 13
Johnson, James, Esq., 21
Johnson, James (turner), 36
Johnson, James, Esq., 37
Johnson, James, Esq., 37
Johnson, James, 38
Johnson, Robert, 37

Johnson, Robert, 37
Johnston, James, Esq., 26
Johnston, Samuel, 14
Jones, J. R., 11
Jones, John R., 18
Jones, John R., 18
Jones, John R., 18
Jones, J. R., 23
Jones, John R., 24
Jones, J. R., 24
Jones, J. R., 24
Jones, J. R., 26
Jones, John R., 29
Jones, John R., 30
Jones, John R., 34
Jones, John R., 35
Jones, John R., 37
Jones, T., 18
Jones, Thomas, 28
Jones, Thomas, 38
Jordan, Ephraim, 20
Jordan, T., 36
Jordon, T., 25
Jordon, Thomas, 38
Kintz, F., 29
Kintz. See also Cuntz
Kirk, Henry, 32
Kuntz. See Cuntz, Kintz
Kuykindall, Abraham, 20
Kuykindall, Abraham, 20
Kuykindall, Abraham, 26
Lachine. See Dudevoir
Lacroix, Jacques, 22
Laderoute, Alexis, 37
Laderoute, Alexis, 37
Lafoy, Vincent, 31
Lafoy, V., 31
Languedoc, Andre, 16
Languedoc, F., 36
Languedoc, Francois, 38
Languedoc, Rene, 12
Languedoc, Rene, 37
Laplante, Jean Baptiste, 17
Latrimouille, J., 20
Latrimouille, Jacques, 38
Latrimouille, Jacques, 38
Ledgerwood, James, 11
Ledgerwood, J., 14
Ledgerwood, James, 20

Ledgerwood, James, 22
Ledgerwood. See Legerwood, 09
Leech, George, 34
Leech, G., 37
Lefeuillade, Joseph, 32
Lefevre, A., widow of, 23
Lefevre, Antoine, dit Chapeau, 38
Lefevre, Charles, 12
Legerwood, James, 09
Legerwood. See Ledgerwood, 09
Legrand, Gabriel, 02
Legrand, Jean M., 38
Legrand, Jean M., 38
Leveron, --, widow, 20
Levine, Joseph, 37
Levine, Joseph, heirs of, 37
Levine, Richard, 38
Lindey, Frederick, 21
Lognon, Francois, 37
Mallett, --, 17
Mallett, Ray, 21
Mallett, L., 21
Mallet, Francis, 29
Mallett, Francis, 30
Marchal, --, 26
Marchal, --, 27
Marchal, Antoine, 26
Marchal, Antoine, 32
Marchal, Antoine, 33
Marchal, Antoine, 33
Marchall, --, 14
Marchall, Antoine, 14
Marie, A., 27
Marshal, John, 34
Marshal, John, 34
Mayes, Jeremiah, 11
Mayo, J., 31
Mays, W., 28
McClure, --, 23
McGowen, --, 22
McGowen, --, 22
McIntosh, William, 17
McIntosh, William, 17
McIntosh, William, 22
McIntosh, William, 30
McIntosh, William, 33
McIntosh, William, 33
Mehl, F., 37
Melton, Thomas, 11

Millburn, Joseph, 34
Mills, William 34
Minor, Isaac, 28
Minor, J., 24
Minor, Jacob, 24
Minor, Jacob, 33
Minor, Jacob, 36
Montplaisir, A., 21
Morrison, William, 27
Morrison, William, 29
Morrison, William, heirs of, 36
Page, William, 09
Page, William, 09
Page, W., 21
Park, --, delegate of this territory, 10
Pea, Henry, 19
Pea, Jacob, 14
Pea, Jacob, 20
Pea, John, 12
Pea, John, 25
Pea, John, 25
Pea, John, 26
Pea, John, 26
Peltier, A., 34
Perrot, Nicholas, 03
Perrot, N., 30
Perrott, Nicholas, 02
Perrott, Nicholas, 03
Perrott, Nicholas, 03
Perrott, Nicholas, 03
Pierre Cornoyer, heirs of, 02
Pipi. See Derozier
Plough, Jacob, 13
Plough, Jacob, 19
Plough, Jacob, 37
Pollard, Richard, 08
Potevin, Jean Baptiste, 05
Price, David, 13
Price, Benjamin D., 13
Price, Benjamin D., 25
Price, Benjamin D., 25
Price, B. D., 35
Price, Benjamin D., 38
Price, Benjamin D., 38
Price, D., 35
Purcell, Andew, 03
Purcell, Jonathan, 03
Purcell, Jonathan, 03
Purcell, William, 03

Querre, Pierre, 02
Querre, Pierre, (son) 03
Querre, Pierre, (father), 03
Querre, Pierre, 03
Querre, Pierre, 03
Querre, Pierre, 03
Querre, Pierre, 03
Racicos, Francis, 19
Racine, Andre, dit Ste. Marie, 24
Racine, Andre, dit Ste. Marie, 34
Racine, Angelique, 04
Racine, Angelique, 04
Racine, Angelique, 04
Racine, Angelique, 04
Racine, Angelique, 05
Racine, Angelique, 05
Racine, Angelique, 06
Racine, Angelique, 07
Racine, Angelique, 07
Racine, Angelique, 07
Racine, Angelique, 10
Racine, Francois, 05
Racine, Francois, 05
Racine, Francois, 06
Racine, Francois, 06
Racine, Francois, 08
Racine, Francois, 10
Racine, Jean Baptiste, 08
Racine, Jean Baptiste, dit Beauchain, 04
Racine, Jean Baptiste, dit Beauchain, 04
Racine, Jean Baptiste, dit Beauchain, 05
Racine, Jean Baptiste, dit Beauchain, 06
Racine, Jean Baptiste, dit Beauchain, 06
Racine, Jean Baptiste, dit Beauchene, 07
Racine, Jean Baptiste, dit Ste. Marie, 07
Ramsay, Al., 13
Reed, B., 36
Reed, William, 11
Reed, W., 20
Reed, --, 25
Reed, William, 31
Reeves, Abner, heirs of, 12
Richardville. See Drouet
Rough, Jacques, 12
Roy, --, 27
Sargent, Winthrop, 05
Sargent, Winthrop, Colonel, 06
Sargent, Winthrop, 06
Sargent, Winthrop, 06

Sargent, [Winthrop], Colonel, 07
Sargent, Winthrop, 07
Sargent, Winthrop, Governor, 10
Simpson, Patrick, 20
Simpson, --, 23
Small, John, 24
Small, John, 35
Smith, Daniel, 12
Smith, D., 33
Snapp, Abraham F.
Snapp, A. F., 12
Snapp, Abraham F., 14
Snapp, Abraham F., 36
St. Clair, Arthur, 08
St. Clair, A[rthur], 08
St. Clair, [Arthur], Governor, 09
Ste. Marie. See Andre Racine
Sturgiss, R., 13
Sullivan, Susan, 17
Thorn, Michael, 11
Thorn, M., 32
Valli, Alexander, 22
Vanderburgh, Henry, 02
Vanderburgh, Henry, 04
Vanderburgh, Henry, 04
Vanderburgh, Henry, 04
Vanderburgh, Henry, 04
Vanderburgh, Henry, 05
Vanderburgh, Henry, 05
Vanderburgh, Henry, 05
Vanderburgh, Henry, 06
Vanderburgh, Henry, 06
Vanderburgh, Henry, 06
Vanderburgh, [Henry], Judge, 07
Vanderburgh, [Henry], Judge, 07
Vanderburgh, Henry, 08
Vanderburgh, Henry, 10
Vanderburgh, Henry, 17
Vanderburgh, Henry, 17
Vanderburgh, Henry, 22
Vanderburgh, Henry, 22
Vanderburgh, Henry, 22
Vanderburgh, Henry, 23
Vanderburgh, Henry, 28
Vaudry, --, 17
Vigo, Francois, 02
Vigo, F., 13
Vigo, F. 16
Vigo, Francis, 18

Vigo, Francis, 22
Vigo, F., 22
Vigo, F., 23
Vigo, Francis, 23
Vigo, Francis, 23
Vigo, Francis, 23
Vigo, Francis, 23
Vigo, Francis, 23
Vigo, F., 27
Vigo, Francis, 29
Vigo, Francis, 29
Vigo, F., 31
Vigo, F., 31
Vigo, F., 31
Vigo, Francis, 33
Vigo, Francis, 33
Vigo, --, 35
Villenaive, --, 17
Viviat, Louis, 01
Wallace, George, Junior, 16
Wallace, George, 16
Westfall, John, 11
Wilkins, A., 14
Williams, Francis, 15
Wyant, Christopher, 18
Wyant, Christopher, 24
Wyant, Christopher, 35
Wyant, Christopher, 35

Selections from **The American State Papers,** No. 3

French and British Land Grants in the

Post Vincennes (Indiana) District

1750-1784
(Continued)

Clifford Neal Smith

First printing, August 1996   rz
Reprint, November 1996   qz

FOREWORD

The American State Papers are official public documents printed privately long before the Congressional Printing Office existed. The printing of public documents during the very early Congresses was done without any general provision of law as to what should be printed. Even as early as 1829 the clerk of the House of Representatives reported that, for the period 1793-1803 not a vestige of manuscript and only a scattered few printed copies were extant. A contributing factor was the destruction of the Capitol building in 1814 by fire.

In 1821 a bill was passed which authorized the publication of 750 copies of all the documents that could be found. The documents were published by two private companies: Gales and Seaton, and Duff Green. Of the two publications, Gales and Seaton is the larger. The Duff Green collection of documents are less comprehensive than the Gales and Seaton collection, and there are many differences in the pagination, particularly in later volumes.

Both publishers appear to have divided the original documents into general subject categories: Foreign Affairs, Indian Affairs, Finance, Commerce and Navigation, Military Affairs, Naval Affairs, Post Office Department, Public Land, and Claim. For genealogical and family history researchers, the last two categories--Public Land and Claims--are the most valuable, and it is from these two categories that this monograph *Selections from* ***The American State Papers*** will be made. The Public Land category, in eight volumes, covers the period 1789-1837; the Claims category, in one volume, covers the period 1790-1823.

In 1972 an attempt was made to index all names in the Public Land and Claims categories of the American State Papers; the index, although monumental, is, however, not complete. All researchers are urged to read pages i through xxvii of

Phillip McMullin, editor, *Grassroots of America: A Computerized Index to the American State Papers: Land Grants and Claims (1789-1837) with Other Aids to Research* (Salt Lake City, Utah: Gendex Corporation, 1972).

The present *Selections from the American State Papers* are the selections, by narrower subject matter, from the Gales and Seaton edition, made by this compiler for the use of genealogists and family historians because the original volumes are now very rare and, no doubt, inaccessible to most researchers.

(ASP 8:1:564)
Supplement to A and C--Continued

Claimants:
 Original: **Laforest, Pierre**
 Present: **Luke Decker, Junior**
50 acres, surveyed; on southeast side of White river, joining **J. Decker**.

Claimants:
 Original: **Leech, Francois**
 Present: **George Leech**
300 acres, surveyed; in the forks of river Des Chis, joining, -- **Harbin**, **R. Johnson**, **T. Jones**, and others.

Claimants:
 Original: **Leech, George**
 Present: **George Leech**
100 acres, surveyed; on south side of White river, on Conger's creek, joining **John Marshal**, and White river.

Claimants:
 Original: **Larsh, Joseph**
 Present: **Robert Gilmore**
68.16 acres, surveyed; on waters of riveer Des Chis, joining -- **Barrackman**.

Claimants:
 Original: **Lognon, Joseph**
 Present: **Jeremiah Claypole**
50 acres, not surveyed.

Claimants:
 Original: **Laframbois, Antoine, dit Gilbeau**
 Present: **Joseph Barron**
68.24 acres, surveyed; in the upper prairie, joining -- **Racine**'s heirs, and **F. Vigo**.

Claimants:
 Original: **Languedoc, Andre**
 Present: **Dubois, Toussaint**
300 acres, surveyed; on southeast side White river, joining heirs of -- **Bosseron**, on Harbin's creek.

Claimants:
 Original: **Leveron, Joseph**
 Present: **Andre Montplaisir**, heirs of
 109.32 acres; surveyed; in the lower prairie, joining **A. Caty** and **Vital Boucher**.

Claimants:
 Original: **Latrimouille, Jacques**
 Present: **Toussaint Dubois**
 163.32 acres, not surveyed.

Claimants:
 Original: **Latrimouille, Jacques**
 Present: not entered
 40.128 acres, not surveyed.

Claimants:
 Original: **Lafevre, Pierre**
 Present: **Toussaint Dubois**
 204 acres, surveyed; on the southeast side of White river, on Chagey's creek.

Claimants:
 Original: **Leveron, Joseph, dit Meteye**
 Present: **Joseph Leveron Meteye**, heirs of
 50 acres, not surveyed.

Claimants:
 Original: **Lionois, Jean Baptiste**, and wife
 Present: **Luke Decker, Esq.**
 68.16 acres, surveyed; on river Des Chis, joining -- **Decoteau** and **J. B. Martin**.

Claimants:
 Original: **Languedoc, Charles**
 Present: **Charles Languedoc**
 171.100 acres, surveyed; in lower prairie, joining **F.? Languedoc** and -- **Bray**.

Claimants:
 Original: **Langlois, Arne***
 Present: **Isaac Decker**, heirs of
 50 acres; surveyed; on south side White river, joining other lands of said Decker. [*so spelled]

Claimants:
Original: **Languedoc, Francois**
Present: **Francois Languedoc**
117.50 acres; surveyed; in lower prairie, joining **Charles Languedoc**.

Claimants:
Original: **Lacoste, Andre**
Present: **Isaac Decker**, heirs of
50 acres, not surveyed.

Claimants:
Original: **Legarde, Jean Baptiste**
Present: **Henry Vanderburgh**
113.16 acres, surveyed; on Mill creek, joining other lands of said Vanderburgh.

Claimants:
Original: **Legarde, Jean Baptiste**
Present: **Francis Vigo**
23.16 acres, surveyed; on Mill creek.

Claimants:
Original: **Lafleur, Jean Baptiste, dit Dutremble**
Present: **Isaac Minor**
50 acres, surveyed; on waters of White river, joining lands of said Minor.

Claimants:
Original: **Lefevre, Antoine**
Present: **William McGowen**
50 acres; surveyed; in the barrens, joining -- **Barrackman** and **C. Wyant**.

Claimants:
Original: **Lacroix, Jacques**
Present: **Robert Buntin**
100 acres, surveyed; on the southeast side of Wabash, joining lands late of **G. B. Dubois**, now Buntin's and vacant land.

Claimants:
Original: **Legrande, Jean M.**
Present: **Abraham Westfall**
300 acres, not surveyed.

Claimants:
 Original: **Legrande, Jean M.**
 Present: **John Lite**
 100 acres; on waters of Marie creek, joining **J. Ockletree** and **J. McClure**.

Claimants:
 Original: **Latrimouille, Jacques**
 Present: **Francis Vigo**
 136.16 acres, surveyed; in the barrens at the Belle Fontaine.

Claimants:
 Original: **Latrimouille, Jacques**
 Present: **Francis Vigo**
 34.12 acres; surveyed; in the upper prairie, joining lands late of **J. Latrimouille**.

Claimants:
 Original: **Latrimouille, Jacques**
 Present: **Robert Buntin**
 34.12 acres, surveyed; on the upper prairie, joining **J. B. Vaudry**.

Claimants:
 Original: **Laforest, Pierre**
 Present: **John R. Jones**
 204 acres, surveyed in part, 171.96 p.[?].

Claimants:
 Original: **Lefevre, Antoine**
 Present: **Francis Vigo**
 27.32 acres, surveyed; in the upper prairie, joining -- **Racine**'s heirs, and **Ja[me]s. Charbonneau**.

Claimants:
 Original: **Lefevre, Antoine**
 Present: **Jean Baptiste Duchesne**, heirs of
 40.144 acres, surveyed; in the upper prairie.

Claimants:
 Original: **Leveron, Joseph, dit Meteye**
 Present: **John Mills**, heirs of
 68.16 acres, not surveyed.

Claimants:
 Original: **Languedoc, Charles**
 Present: **Daniel Hazleton**
 50 acres, not surveyed.

Claimants:
 Original: **Mehl, Frederick**
 Present: **Frederick Mehl**
 300 acres, surveyed; in the barrens, bounded by **F. Mehl, F. Lognon,** and the commons.

Claimants:
 Original: **Murphy, John**
 Present: **Daniel Smith**
 300 acres, surveyed; including the old Indian village on waters of Marie creek, joining -- **Ledgerwood**.

Claimants:
 Original: **Mays, William**
 Present: **William Mays**
 200 acres, surveyed; on northwest side of White river, bounded by -- **Decker, F. Biddle**, and said Mays.

Claimants:
 Original: **Mays Jeremiah**
 Present: **Jeremiah Mays**
 200 acres, surveyed; on northwest side of Whte river, bounded by -- **P. Frederick, William Reed**, and vacant lands.

Claimants:
 Original: **Matson, Ralph**
 Present: **William Reed**
 400 acres, surveyed; on waters of White river, bounded by **J. Mays,** widow -- **Wilson** and other lands of said Reed.

Claimants:
 Original: **Meuville, Joseph**
 Present: **Adam Harness**
 50 acres, surveyed; on southeast side Wabash, at the Little Rock joining other lands of said Harness.

Claimants:
 Original: **Mallett, Antoine**
 Present: **John Baptiste Delaurier**
 68.16 acres, surveyed; in Cathelinette prairie, joining other lands of said Delaurier.

Claimants:
 Original: **Mallett, Francois**
 Present: **Benjamin Beckes**
 136.16 acres, surveyed; on river Des Chis, joining other lands of said Beckes.

6

Claimants:
 Original: **Martin, John**
 Present: **John Martin**
 300 acres, surveyed; on northwest side of White river, joining **P. Beckes** and heirs of **W. Morrison**.

Claimants:
 Original: **Mays, Robert**
 Present: **Robert Mays**, heirs of
 100 acres, surveyed; between Des Chis and White rivers, joining Matson's Station.

(ASP 8:1:565)

Claimants:
 Original: **Mallett, Francois**
 Present: **Joshua Harbin**, heirs of
 136.16 acres, surveyed; on river Des Chis, joining other lands of said Harbin.

Claimants:
 Original: **Mallett, Francois**
 Present: **Francois Mallett**, heirs of
 89.14 acres, surveyed; in lower prairie, joining **C. Dudevoir** and **C. Bonn**.

Claimants:
 Original: **Mallett, Francois**
 Present: **Francois Mallett**, heirs of
 136.16 acres, not surveyed; granted at the Faux Chenal.

Claimants:
 Original: **Montplaisir, Andre**
 Present: **William H. Harrison**
 118.143 acres, surveyed; below the lower prairie, on the Wabash.

Claimants:
 Original: **Marie, --**, widow of
 Present: **Toussaint Dubois**
 50 acres, surveyed; on the south side Embarras, joining other lands of said Dubois.

Claimants:
 Original: **Mallett, Louis**
 Present: **Joseph** and **Louis Mallett**
 68.24 acres, surveyed; in lower prairie, joining **N. Chapard**.

Claimants:
 Original: **Martin, John**
 Present: **Thomas Coulter**
 68.24 acres, surveyed; in Cathelinette prairie, joining **P. Simpson**.

Claimants:
 Original: **Marie, Antoine**
 Present: **Jean Baptiste Bonhomme**
 35.70 acres, surveyed; in lower prairie, joining -- **Villeneuve** and **F. Hamtramck**.

Claimants:
 Original: **Mallett, Pierre**
 Present: **Isaac Decker**, heirs of
 50 acres, surveyed; on south side of White river, joining other lands of said Decker.

Claimants:
 Original: **Marie, Antoine**
 Present: **William McIntosh**
 102.24 acres, surveyed; in lower prairie, joining heirs of **B. Danis** and **G. Page**, [donation land] No. 8.

Claimants:
 Original: **McNulty, James**
 Present: **Robert Buntin**
 22.114 acres, surveyed; in Cathelinette prairie, joining **J. Tougas** and **J. Martin**.

Claimants:
 Original: **Meteye, Levron, Louis**
 Present: **Christopher Wyant**
 136.35 acres, surveyed; on waters of Mill creek, joining said Wyant.

Claimants:
 Original: **Millett, Jean Baptiste**
 Present: **Susan Sullivan**
 68.16 acres, surveyed; in river Des Chis prairie, joining **Luke Decker**.

Claimants:
 Original: **Noye, Jacob**
 Present: **Jacob Noye**, heirs of
 200 acres, not surveyed.

Claimants:
 Original: **Ouilette, Jean Baptiste**
 Present: **Antoine Marshal**
 102.24 acres, surveyed; on waters of Mill creek, joining **A. F. Snapp**

Claimants:
 Original: **Petit, Antoine, dit Lalemier**
 Present: **Antoine Lalemier**
 68.16 acres, surveyed; below the lower prairie, bounded by **N. Chapard** and **A. Gamelin**.

Claimants:
 Original: **Petit, Antoine, dit Lalemier**
 Present: **Toussaint Dubois**
 51.12 acres, not to be surveyed. More conveyed by Lalemier than the old grant amounted to, on Wabash, below lower prairies, joining **Antoine Gamelin**.

Claimants:
 Original: **Pea, Jacob**
 Present: **John Pea**
 300 acres, surveyed; on southeast side of White river, on Conger's creek, joining **P. Catt**.

Claimants:
 Original: **Page, Guillaume**
 Present: **Adam Harness**
 50 acres, surveyed; on southeast side of Wabash, at the Little Rock, joining other lands of Harness.

Claimants:
 Original: **Pancake, Joseph**
 Present: **Abraham Huff**
 300 acres, surveyed; on waters of Marie creek, joining **B. D. Price**.

Claimants:
 Original: **Pea, Daniel**
 Present: **Daniel Pea**
 300 acres, surveyed; on northwest side of White river, joining other lands of.

Claimants:
 Original: **Peltier, Andrew**
 Present: **Abner Reeves**, heirs of
 50 acres, surveyed; on northwest side of Wabash, bounded by the river, and **A. F. Snapp**.

Claimants:
 Original: **Peltier, Eustace**
 Present: **Toussaint Dubois**
 34.8 acres, surveyed; in the lower prairie, joining -- **Querrie** and -- **Cartier**.

Claimants:
 Original: **Perron, Pierre**
 Present: **Toussaint Dubois**
 136.16 acres, not surveyed.

Claimants:
 Original: **Perron, Pierre**, or **Jean Baptiste [Perron]**
 Present: **Toussaint Dubois**
 136.16 acres, not surveyed.

Claimants:
 Original: **Pillars, Richard**
 Present: **Parmenas Beckes**
 300 acres, surveyed; on river Des Chis, joining said Beckes, and **J. Martin**.

Claimants:
 Original: **Pappino, Peter**
 Present: **Luke Decker, Esq.**
 340.44 acres, surveyed; on river Des Chis, joining **B. Beckes**.

Claimants:
 Original: **Parent, Joachim**
 Present: **Susan Sullivan**
 68.24 acres, surveyed; in Cathelinette prairie, joining **P. Laforest**, No. 1.

Claimants:
 Original: **Pluchon, Louis**
 Present: **William McIntosh**
 136.16 acres, not surveyed; granted five miles south of Vincennes.

Claimants:
 Original: **Page, Guillaume**
 Present: **Andre Desbiens**
 51.11 acres, not surveyed; below the lower prairie, joining lands late of **A. Petit** and **J. F. Rivet**.

Claimants:
 Original: **Page, Guillaume**
 Present: **Francis Vigo**
 25.80 acres, not surveyed; below the lower prairie.

Claimants:
 Original: **Page, Joseph**
 Present: **Francis Vigo**
 136.16 acres, not surveyed; granted on Embarras, at the black ground.

Claimants:
 Original: **Page, William**
 Present: **Francis Vigo**
 136.16 acres, not surveyed; granted on Embarras, at the black ground.

Claimants:
 Original: **Pea, John**
 Present: **James Ledgerwood**
 200 acres, surveyed; on Bosseron [Creek] joining.

Claimants:
 Original: **Pearou, Amable**
 Present: **Thomas Barton**
 204 acres, surveyed; on the side of White river, about two miles above Harbin's ferry.

Claimants:
 Original: **Paine, Louis**
 Present: **Louis Paine**
 136.16 acres, not surveyed.

Claimants:
 Original: **Perrot, Nicholas**
 Present: **John R. Jones**
 136.16 acres, surveyed; on the Wabash, at the Little Rock, joining **D. Smith, F. Dubois,** and others.

Claimants:
 Original: **Pedoret, Joseph, Junior**
 Present: **Susan Sullivan**
 68.16 acres, surveyed; on the river Des Chis prairie.

Claimants:
 Original: **Park, William**
 Present: **William Park**
 68.16 acres, surveyed; in lower prairie, joining -- **Richardville** and **P. Cartier**, No. 20.

Claimants:
 Original: **Page, William**
 Present: **James Ledgerwood**
 340 acres, surveyed; on Bosseron creek.

Claimants:
 Original: **Querrie, Pierre**
 Present: **Abraham F. Snapp**
 68.16 acres, surveyed; on the east side of Mill creek, joining **R. Buntin** and **A. Marshal**.

Claimants:
 Original: **Querrie, Pierre**
 Present: **Jarvis Hazelton**
 50 acres, not surveyed; granted on south side White river, joining the militia line; no lines to be found.

Claimants:
 Original: **Racine, Jean Baptiste**
 Present: **Paul & Marguerite Gamelin**, heirs of
 68.24 acres, surveyed; in the upper prairie, boundedc by **M. Brouellette** and **A. Lefevre**.

Claimants:
 Original: **Robbins, John**
 Present: **John Robbins**, heirs of
 300 acres; surveyed; on waters of river Des Chis, joining **John Harbin** and **John Wilmore**.

Claimants:
 Original: **Richard, Marie**
 Present: **Antoine Marshal**
 127.95 acres, surveyed; at the Little Rock on the Wabash.

Claimants:
 Original: **Richard, Marie**
 Present: **Abraham F. Snapp**
 85.16 acres, surveyed; at the Little Rock on the Wabash.

Claimants:
 Original: **Richard, Marie**
 Present: U. S. Garrison
85.16 acres; surveyed; at the Little Rock, on the Wabash.

Claimants:
 Original: **Racine, Francois**
 Present: **Patrick Simpson**
280.155 acres, surveyed in part; on waters of Mill creek, joining -- **Vigo**, other lands of said Simpson, vacant lands, prairie lots.

Claimants:
 Original: **Ramsay, Allen**
 Present: **Luke Decker, Esq.**
85.10 acres, surveyed; on north side White river, joining **A. Petit** and said Decker.

Claimants:
 Original: **Racine, Jean Baptiste**
 Present: **Toussaint Dubois**
136.16 acres, surveyed; on the Wabash, joining **Josh. Lamotte** and -- **Hunot**.

Claimants:
 Original: **Racine St. Marie, Francois**
 Present: **Isaac Decker**, heirs of
50 acres, surveyed; on south side of White river, joining other lands of said Decker.

(ASP 8:1:566)

Claimants:
 Original: **Racine, Jean Baptiste**
 Present: **Joseph Lamotte**, heirs of
136.16 acres, surveyed; on north side of Wabash, joining -- **Dubois** and **A. Racine**.

Claimants:
 Original: **Ravalet, Louis**
 Present: **William McIntosh**
136.16 acres, not surveyed; granted six miles southwest of Vincennes.

Claimants:
 Original: **Roy, Andre**
 Present: **William Morrison**
 68.16 acres, surveyed; in lower prairie, joining **T. Dubois and N. Chapard.**

Claimants:
 Original: **Racine, Francois**
 Present: **Angelique Racine**
 136.16 acres, not surveyed.

Claimants:
 Original: **Ravalet, Jean Baptiste**
 Present: **Christopher Wyant**
 50 acres, not surveyed; located one mile below the forks of White river on west side Wabash joining same.

Claimants:
 Original: **Robinson, Andrew**
 Present: **Abraham F. Snapp**
 136.16 acres, surveyed; on north side of Wabash river, joining heirs of **A. Reeves.**

Claimants:
 Original: **Richard, --, dit Antaya,** widow
 Present: **William McIntosh**
 68.16 acres, not surveyed.

Claimants:
 Original: **Smith, Daniel**
 Present: **Daniel Smith**
 100 acres, surveyed; on river Marie, including the Old village.

Claimants:
 Original: **Smith, Daniel**
 Present: **Isaac White**
 100 acres; surveyed; on river Des Chis, bounded by -- **Leech** and others.

Claimants:
 Original: **Spech, Henry**
 Present: **Isaac Minor**
 136.16 acres, not surveyed; granted at the Little village.

Claimants:
 Original: **St. Dezier, --,** heirs of
 Present: **Edward Purcell**
 50 acres, not surveyed.

Claimants:
 Original: **Selby, Thomas**
 Present: **William Reed**
250 acres, surveyed; on the waters of White river, joining other lands of said Reed.

Claimants:
 Original: **Small, John**
 Present: **John Ockletree**
310.41 acres, surveyed; on waters of Marie creek, joining the donation tract.

Claimants:
 Original: **Snapp, Abraham F.**
 Present: **Abraham F. Snapp**
300 acres, surveyed; on Bosseron creek.

Claimants:
 Original: **St. Aubin, Joseph**
 Present: **Abraham Kuykindall**
50 acres, surveyed; on White river, joining said Kuykindall.

Claimants:
 Original: **Slaughter, Lawrence**
 Present: **William H. Harrison**
136.16 acres, surveyed; on the north side of Wabash, joining lands of said Harrison.

Claimants:
 Original: **Seguin, Alexis**
 Present: **Toussaint Dubois**
50 acres, surveyed; opposite Harbin's ferry, on the southeast side of White river.

Claimants:
 Original: **Savage, John**
 Present: **George Fidler**
136.16 acres, surveyed; on White river, joining the heirs of **George Berger**.

Claimants:
 Original: **Simpson, Patrick**
 Present: **Thomas Coulter**
45.70 acres, surveyed; in Cathelinette prairie, joining **J. Tougas** and **John Martin**.

Claimants:
 Original: **Sullivan, Susan**
 Present: **Daniel Sullivan**
 300 acres, not surveyed.

Claimants:
 Original: **St. Marie, Etienne**
 Present: **William McIntosh**
 400 acres, surveyed; at the Grand rapids, on the west side of Wabash.

Claimants:
 Original: **St. Aubin, Jean Baptiste**
 Present: **Henry Vanderburgh**
 68.16 acres, surveyed; in the upper prairie, joining **R. Buntin** and other lands of said Vanderburgh.

Claimants:
 Original: **St. Marie, Francois**
 Present: **Henry Vanderburgh**
 400 acres, surveyed; at the Grand rapids, on the west of the Wabash.

Claimants:
 Original: **Small, Thomas**
 Present: **James Ledgerwood**
 340.44 acres, surveyed; on Bosseron creek, joining.

Claimants:
 Original: **Souci, --**
 Present: **Toussaint Dubois**
 50 acres, not surveyed.

Claimants:
 Original: **St. Auge, Joseph, dit Haintonge**
 Present: **Antoine Drouet, dit Richardville**
 68.8 acres, surveyed; in the lower prairie, joining **S. Delaurier** and **-- Querre**, No. 19,

Claimants:
 Original: **Thorn, Charles**
 Present: **William Martin**
 100 acres, not surveyed.

Claimants:
 Original: **Thorn, Charles**
 Present: **Charles Thorn**
 200 acres, surveyed; on waters of Wilson's creek, bounded by heirs of **F. Bosseron**.

Claimants:
 Original: **Thorn, Michael, Senior**
 Present: **Charles** and **Jacob Thorn**
 340.40 acres, surveyed; on the waters of river Des Chis, bounded by **J. R. Jones** [and] **M. Asturgas**.

Claimants:
 Original: **Thorn, Michael, Junior**
 Present: **Michael Thorn**
 250 acres, surveyed; two hundred acres on White river and fifty on river Des Chis, respectively bounded by **J. Decker, Junior**, and **A. Westfall**.

Claimants:
 Original: **Thorn, Peter**
 Present: **Benjamin D. Price**
 200 acres, surveyed; on the waters of Marie creek, bounded by lands of B. D. Price.

Claimants:
 Original: **Thorn, Daniel**
 Present: **Robert Asturgas**
 250 acres, surveyed; on waters of Bosseron creek, bounded by **F. Berger**, **J. Ledgerwood**, and **J. Davis**.

Claimants:
 Original: **Tougas, Joseph**
 Present: **Abraham F. Snapp**
 50 acres, surveyed; on Small's creek, joining other lands of said Snapp.

Claimants:
 Original: **Tevebaugh, Jacob, Junior**
 Present: **Jacob Tevebaough, Junior**, heirs of
 200 acres, not surveyed.

Claimants:
 Original: **Thorn, Jacob**
 Present: **Isaac Decker**, heirs of
 150 acres, surveyed; on southeast side of White river, joining the militia tract.

Claimants:
Original: **Tougas, Joseph**
Present: **Francis Vigo**
255 acres, not surveyed; granted on the river Embarras, at the black ground.

Claimants:
Original: **Valli, Alexander**
Present: **Alexander Valli**
68.16 acres, surveyed; in lower prairie.

Claimants:
Original: **Valli, Alexander**
Present: **William Bullett**
68.16 acres, surveyed; in lower prairie.

Claimants:
Original: **Vigo, Francis**
Present: **William H. Harrison**
49.25 acres, surveyed; in the Indian Fields, joining the town of Vincennes.

Claimants:
Original: **Valli, Alexander**
Present: **Jeremiah Claypole**
50 acres, not surveyed.

Claimants:
Original: **Vaudry, Jean Baptiste**
Present: **Toussaint Dubois**
50 acres, surveyed; on the southeast side of White river, joining other lands of said Dubois.

Claimants:
Original: **Vaudry, Jean Baptiste**, widow of
Present: **Toussaint Dubois**
340.44 acres, surveyed; on the west? side of Embarras river, joining other lands of said Dubois.

Claimants:
Original: Vincennes, church
Present: Church wardens
136.16 acres, surveyed; in lower prairie, joining the village.

Claimants:
Original: **Villeneuve, Charles**
Present: **Charles Villeneuve**, heirs of
95.112 acres, surveyed; in lower prairie, joining **Alexander Valli**.

Claimants:
 Original: **Vaudry, Jean Baptiste**
 Present: **Antoine Drouet, dit Richardville**
 37.75 acres, surveyed; in the lower prairie.

Claimants:
 Original: **Villeray, Jean Baptiste**
 Present: **William McIntosh**
 136.16 acres, not surveyed; granted on Embarras river, at the black ground.

Claimants:
 Original: **Valli, Alexander**
 Present: **Alexander Valli**
 136.16 acres, surveyed; on northwest side of Wabash, at the river Natte, joining lands of -- **Dubois**.

Claimants:
 Original: **Villeneuve, Charles**
 Present: **George Wallace, Junior**
 136.16 acres, not surveyed.

Claimants:
 Original: **Vaudry, Jean Baptiste**
 Present: **Jean F. Hamtramck**, heirs of
 68.16 acres, surveyed; in the lower prairie, joining land late of **T. Dubois**.

Claimants:
 Original: **Vigo, Francis**
 Present: **Nicholas Cardinal**, heirs of
 68.16 acres, surveyed; in the upper prairie, joining lands late of **M. Brouillett** and **P. Conoyer**.

Claimants:
 Original: **Vigo, Francis**
 Present: **Francis Vigo**
 136.16 acres, surveyed; on the northwest side of Wabash, joining lands late of -- **Hunot**.

Claimants:
 Original: **Vigo, Francis**
 Present: **Francis Vigo**
 136.16 acres, not surveyed; granted on the north side of the Wabash, joining other lands of said Vigo.

Claimants:
 Original: **Vaudry, Jean Baptiste**
 Present: **Francis Vigo**
 68.24 acres, surveyed; in the upper prairie, joining **J. Chartier**.

Claimants:
 Original: **Valli, Alexander**
 Present: **Alexander Valli, Junior**
 100.140 acres, surveyed; in lower prairie bounded by -- **Villeneuve** and -- **Dagneau**.

Claimants:
 Original: **Vaudry, Jean Baptiste**
 Present: **Andrew Wilkins**
 206 acres, surveyed; in the forks of Marie creek, joining **John Widner**.

Claimants:
 Original: **Vachette, Pierre A.**
 Present: not entered
 50 acres, not surveyed.

Claimants:
 Original: **Westfall, Abraham**
 Present: **John Widner**
 300 acres, surveyed; in the forks of Marie creek, joining **A. Wilkins**, etc.

Claimants:
 Original: **Wilson, Alexander**
 Present: **Alexander Wilson**, heirs of
 120 acres, surveyed; on the south side of White river, bounded by **J. Wilson**, **P. Catt**, and **J. Pea**.

Claimants:
 Original: **Wilson, Alexander**
 Present: **Alexander Wilson**, heirs of
 180 acres, surveyed; on waters of White river, bounded by -- **Pea**, -- **Reed**, **R. Mays**, and **M. Decker**.

Claimants:
 Original: **Wilmore, John**
 Present: **John Wilmore**
 216 acres, surveyed; on waters of river Des Chis, bounded by **Julia Robins** and **A.? Westfall**.

Claimants:
 Original: **Wilmore, John**
 Present: **Thomas Anderson**
 134 acres, surveyed; on river Marie, joining **B. D. Price**.

Claimants:
 Original: **Wyant, Christopher**
 Present: **John Stilwell**
 400 acres, surveyed; on the Wabash, joining **T. Dubois**.

Claimants:
 Original: **Watkins, Samuel**
 Present: **Luke Decker, Esq.**
 136.16 acres, surveyed; on river Des Chis, joining the Cedar swamp.

Claimants:
 Original: **Westfall, John**
 Present: **William Bullett**
 300 acres, not surveyed.

Claimants:
 Original: **Wilson, Francis**
 Present: **Francis Wilson**
 400 acres, not surveyed.

Claimants:
 Original: **Delorie, Louis**
 Present: not entered with the Register
 136 acres, not surveyed; in the prairie of the Horse-shoe swamp.

(ASP 8:1:568)

List of Lands confirmed by the different
Governors in virtue of Militia rights.
Those with a number affixed are surveyed in a body
on the southeast side of White river.

Claimants:
 Original: **Andre, Pierre**
 Present: **Christopher Wyant**
 -- acres, not surveyed.

Claimants:
 Original: **Barrois, Lambert**
 Present: **Noah Spears**
Tract 47, not surveyed.

Claimants:
 Original: **Bonhomme, Jean Baptiste**
 Present: **Daniel Smith**
Tract 84, not surveyed.

Claimants:
 Original: **Baird, Thomas**
 Present: **Adam Harness**
--, surveyed; on Wabash, opposite the Little rapids, joining lands of **J. Plough** and other lands of Harness.

Claimants:
 Original: **Boyer, Jean Baptiste** or **Toussaint [Boyer?]**
 Present: **Jarvis Hazleton**
Tract 32.

Claimants:
 Original: **Bolon, Amable**
 Present: **Robert Falls**
Tract 107.

Claimants:
 Original: **Baird, Joseph**
 Present: **Elias Biddle**
--, surveyed; on waters of White river, joining **John Martin** and **Jesse Thomas**.

Claimants:
 Original: **Bordeleau, Charles**
 Present: **Abraham Decker, Senior**
--, surveyed; on south side of White river, joining **L. T. Denoyon**.

Claimants:
 Original: **Barron, Joseph**
 Present: **Abraham Kuykindall**
--, surveyed; on White river, joining other lands of said Kuykindall.

Claimants:
 Original: **Boucher, Joseph**
 Present: **Abraham Kuykindall**
--, surveyed; on White river, joining other lands of said Kuykindall.

Claimants:
 Original: **Beaudoin, Benjamin**
 Present: **John Pea**
--, surveyed; on southeast side of White river, joining **W. Wilson,** and other lands of said Pea.

Claimants:
 Original: **Brouillet, Michael**
 Present: **Toussaint Dubois**
Tract 116.

Claimants:
 Original: **Barrois, Leon**
 Present: **Toussaint Dubois**
Tract 58.

Claimants:
 Original: **Boyer, Francois**
 Present: **Toussaint Dubois**
Tract 53.

Claimants:
 Original: **Bolon, Gabriel, Junior**
 Present: **Toussaint Dubois**
Not surveyed.

Claimants:
 Original: **Baird, Robert**
 Present: **John Bailey**
Not surveyed.

Claimants:
 Original: **Beckes, Benjamin**
 Present: **John Mills,** heirs of
Tract 102.

Claimants:
 Original: **Barsaleau*, Jean Baptiste**
 Present: **William McIntosh**
Tract 69. [*so spelled]

Claimants:
 Original: **Berger, Frederick**
 Present: **Francis Vigo**
 --, surveyed; on waters of Mill creek, joining -- **Buntin**, -- **Johnson**, and -- **Wyant**.

Claimants:
 Original: **Barrackman, Christopher**
 Present: **Christopher Barrackman**, heirs of
 Tract 38.

Claimants:
 Original: **Barrackman, Abraham**
 Present: **Abraham Barrackman**
 Tract 122.

Claimants:
 Original: **Berger, Peter**
 Present: **Henry Pea**
 Tract 74.

Claimants:
 Original: **Berger, George**
 Present: **John Davis**
 --, surveyed; on Bosseron [creek], joining -- **Ledgerwood** and other lands of said Davis.

Claimants:
 Original: **Bino, Jean Baptiste**
 Present: **Christopher Wyant**
 --, surveyed; on the waters of Mill creek, joining said Wyant.

Claimants:
 Original: **Bordeleau, Antoine** or **Francois**
 Present: not entered
 Tract 24.

Claimants:
 Original: **Bordeleau, Pierre**
 Present: not entered
 Tract 25.

Claimants:
 Original: **Boneau, Nicholas**
 Present: **David Robb**
 Tract 31.

Claimants:
 Original: **Bolon, Gabriel, Senior**
 Present: not entered

Claimants:
 Original: **Barrois, Alexis,** heirs of
 Present: not entered
 --, surveyed; on waters of river Des Chis, at the Stone Chimney.

Claimants:
 Original: **Baird, Thomas**
 Present: not entered
 --, surveyed.

Claimants:
 Original: **Chabert, Pierre**
 Present: **Laurent Bazadon**
 Tract 27.

Claimants:
 Original: **Cardinal, Toussaint**
 Present: **Noah Spears**
 Tract 54.

Claimants:
 Original: **Charbonneau, Germain**
 Present: **Adam Harness**
 --. surveyed; on southeast side Wabash, opposite the Little Rock, joining other lands of said Harness.

Claimants:
 Original: **Coder, Andre, Junior**
 Present: **Joseph Foreman**
 Tract 40.

Claimants:
 Original: **Cambris, Andre**
 Present: **Thomas Jones**
 Tract 64.

Claimants:
 Original: **Cloud, Joseph**
 Present: **Henry Kirk**
 Tract 104.

Claimants:
 Original: **Chatignie, Ignace**
 Present: **Moses Decker, Junior**
 Tract 125.

Claimants:
 Original: **Coder, Jean Baptiste**
 Present: **Thomas Holder**
--, surveyed; on waters of Bosseron [creek], joining said Holder and **James Ledgerwood**.

Claimants:
 Original: **Coder, Louis**
 Present: **David Robb**
 Tract 34.

Claimants:
 Original: **Cartier, Pierre, Junior**
 Present: **John Ockletree**
--, surveyed; on waters of Marie creek, joining other lands of said Ockletree.

Claimants:
 Original: **Cantelmy, Francois**
 Present: **John Harbin**
--, surveyed; on river Des Chis, joining other lands of John Harbin.

Claimants:
 Original: **Catt, Philip**
 Present: **Philip Catt**
--, surveyed; on water of river Des Chis, joining **Abraham Decker**.

Claimants:
 Original: **Chartran, Jean Baptiste**
 Present: **Francis Williams**
--, surveyed; on the high ground between Bosseron and Marie creeks.

Claimants:
 Original: **Clermont, Pierre**
 Present: **William McIntosh**
 Tract 120.

Claimants:
 Original: **Coder, Toussaint, Junior**
 Present: **William Morrison**
 Tract 62.

Claimants:
 Original: **Coder, Andre, Senior**
 Present: **Henry Vanderburgh**
 Tract 55.

Claimants:
 Original: **Coder, Henry**
 Present: **Henry Vanderburgh**
 Tract 30.

Claimants:
 Original: **Courtois, Pierre**
 Present: **Zachariah Mills**
 Tract 123.

Claimants:
 Original: **Chartier, Michael**
 Present: **Robert Buntin**
 --, surveyed; on waters of Mill creek, joining **J[ame]s Johnson, F. Berger**, and **P. Simpson**.

Claimants:
 Original: **Campeau, Pierre**
 Present: **Abraham Stepp***
 Tract 79.   [*so spelled]

Claimants:
 Original: **Capucine, Theodore**
 Present: **Abraham Stepp**
 Tract 82.

Claimants:
 Original: **Compagnotte, Pierre**
 Present: **Henry Pea**
 Tract 73.

Claimants:
 Original: **Cheroqui, Jean Baptiste**
 Present: **John Mills**, heirs of
 Tract 121.

Claimants:
 Original: **Cornoyer, Alexis**
 Present: not entered
 Tract 8.

Claimants:
 Original: **Coder, Pierre**
 Present: not entered
 Tract 77.

Claimants:
 Original: **Chabotte, Joseph, Junior**
 Present: **John Johnson**
 Tract 37.

Claimants:
 Original: **Dumay, Francois**
 Present: **Adam Harness**
 --, surveyed; on White river, bounded by **A. Ramsay, T. Decker** and White river.

Claimants:
 Original: **Depron, Bernard**
 Present: **Noah Spears**
 Tract 50.

Claimants:
 Original: **Dagenet, Ambroise**
 Present: **Daniel Smith**
 Tract 80.

Claimants:
 Original: **Decker, Moses, Senior**
 Present: **Moses Decker, Senior**
 --, surveyed; on waters of river Des Chis, bounded by said Decker and **Luke Decker**.

Claimants:
 Original: **Dejean, Philip**
 Present: **Thomas Jones**
 --, not surveyed.

Claimants:
 Original: **Decker, Joseph, Senior**
 Present: **Ephraim Jordon**
 -- surveyed; on waters of White river, joining heirs of **George Berger**.

Claimants:
 Original: **Dubois, Toussaint**
 Present: **Elias Biddle**
 --, surveyed; on waters of White river, bounded by **F. Jordon, J[ame]s Johnson**, and **D. Pea**.

Claimants:
 Original: **Denoyon, Louis Toussaint**
 Present: **Abraham Decker, Senior**
 --, surveyed.

Claimants:
 Original: **Denoyon, Louis**
 Present: **Toussaint Dubois**
 Tract 17.

Claimants:
 Original: **Denoyon, Louis**
 Present: **Toussaint Dubois**
 Tract 45.

Claimants:
 Original: **Devore, Philip**
 Present: **James Robb**
 Tract 56.

Claimants:
 Original: **Dumais, Jean Baptiste**
 Present: **John Harbin**
 --, surveyed; on river Des Chis, joining heirs of **John Robbins**, **P. Barrackman**.

Claimants:
 Original: **Duquindre, Jean Baptiste**
 Present: **Abraham F. Snapp**
 Tract 128.

Claimants:
 Original: **Dumais, Jacques**
 Present: **Michael Dace**
 Tract 49.

Claimants:
 Original: **Dubois, Joseph**
 Present: **Abraham Kuykindall**
 --, surveyed; on White river, joining other lands of said Kuykindall.

Claimants:
 Original: **Deneau, Pierre**
 Present: **Robert Warth**
 --, not surveyed.

Claimants:
 Original: **Day, Robert**
 Present: **Robert Day**
 Tract 26.

Claimants:
 Original: **Decker, Isaac**
 Present: **Thomas Anderson**
 Tract 119.

Claimants:
 Original: **Decker, Luke, Esq.**
 Present: **Luke Decker, Esq.**
 --, surveyed; on river Des Chis, joining said Decker.

Claimants:
 Original: **Decker, John**
 Present: not surveyed

Claimants:
 Original: **Decker, Abraham, Junior**
 Present: **Abraham Decker**
 Tract 54.

Claimants:
 Original: **Dudevoir, Charles, dit Lachine**
 Present: **John Gibson, Senior**
 --, surveyed; on waters of Mill creek, joining said Gibson and **James Johnson.**

Claimants:
 Original: **Dubois, Jean Baptiste**
 Present: **John Mills,** heirs of
 Tract 33.

Claimants:
 Original: **Decker, Tobias**
 Present: **Isaac Decker,** heirs of
 -- surveyed; on southeast side of White river, joining other lands of said Decker.

Claimants:
 Original: **Dielle, Charles, Junior**
 Present: **Henry Vanderburgh**
 Tract 12.

Claimants:
 Original: **Deganne, Joseph**
 Present: **John Mills**, heirs of
 Tract 117.

Claimants:
 Original: **Dapron, Pierre**
 Present: **John Davis**
 Tract 127.

Claimants:
 Original: **Dapron, Joseph**
 Present: not entered

Claimants:
 Original: **Depre, Francois**
 Present: not entered.
 Not surveyed.

Claimants:
 Original: **Decker, Moses**
 Present: not entered
 Not surveyed.

Claimants:
 Original: **Edeline, Joseph**
 Present: **Zachariah Mills**
 Tract 124.

Claimants:
 Original: **Edeline, Nicholas**
 Present: **William McIntosh**
 Tract 67.

Claimants:
 Original: **Frederick, Lewis**
 Present: **Lewis Frederick**
 --, surveyed; on Muddy run, bounded by **P. Devore, F. Lindey,** and **Seb[astian] Frederick**.

Claimants:
 Original: **Frederick, Sebastian**
 Present: **Sebastian Frederick**
 --, surveyed; on Muddy run, bounded by **F. Lindey** and **P. Devore**.

Claimants:
 Original: **Frichette, Jean Baptiste**
 Present: **Henry Kirk**
 Tract 105.

Claimants:
 Original: **Fortin, Jean Belony**
 Present: **John Stilwell**
 Not surveyed.

Claimants:
 Original: **Faucher, Pierre**
 Present: **John Vanderburgh**
 Tract 103.

Claimants:
 Original: **Frederick, Peter**
 Present: not entered

Claimants:
 Original: **Guitarre, Jean Baptiste**
 Present: **Jacob Tevebaugh**
 Tract 61.

Claimants:
 Original: **Grimarre, Pierre**
 Present: **Joseph Foreman**
 Tract 39.

Claimants:
 Original: **Gregoire, Joseph**
 Present: **Ebenezer Sevans**
 Tract 83.

SURNAME INDEX

Anderson, Thomas, 20
Anderson, Thomas, 29
Andre, Pierre, 20
Antaya. See -- Richard
Asturgas, M., 16
Asturgas, Robert, 16
Bailey, John, 22
Baird, Joseph, 21
Baird, Robert, 22
Baird, Thomas, 21
Baird, Thomas, 24
Barrackman, --, 1
Barrackman, --, 3
Barrackman, Abraham, 23
Barrackman, Christopher, 23
Barrackman, Christopher, heirs of, 23
Barrackman, P., 28
Barrois, Alexis, heirs of, 24
Barrois, Lambert, 21
Barrois, Leon, 22
Barron, Joseph, 1
Barron, Joseph, 21
Barsaleau, Jean Baptiste, 22
Barton, Thomas, 10
Bazadon, Laurent, 24
Beaudoin, Benjamin, 22
Beckes, Benjamin, 5
Beckes, Benjamin, 22
Beckes, Benjamin, 22
Beckes, B., 9
Beckes, Parmenas, 9
Belony. See Jean Fortin
Berger, F., 16
Berger, F., 26
Berger, Frederick, 23
Berger, George, 14
Berger, George, 23
Berger, Geroge, 27
Berger, Peter, 23
Biddle, Elias, 21
Biddle, Elias, 27
Biddle, F., 5
Bino, Jean Baptiste, 23
Bolon, Amable, 21
Bolon, Gabriel, Junior, 22
Bolon, Gabriel, Senior, 24

Boneau, Nicholas, 23
Bonhomme, Jean Baptiste, 7
Bonhomme, Jean Baptiste, 21
Bonn, C., 6
Bordeleau, Antoine, 23
Bordeleau, Charles, 21
Bordeleau, Francois, 23
Bordeleau, Pierre, 23
Bosseron, --, heirs of, 1
Bosseron, F., 16
Boucher, Joseph, 22
Boucher, Vital, 2
Boyer, Francois, 22
Boyer, Jean Baptiste, 21
Boyer, Toussaint, 21
Bray, --, 2
Brouellette, M., 11
Brouillet, Michael, 22
Brouillett, M., 18
Bullett, William, 17
Bullett, William, 20
Buntin, Robert, 3
Buntin, Robert, 4
Buntin, Robert, 7
Buntin, Rober, 26
Buntin, R., 11
Buntin, R., 15
Buntin, --, 23
Cambris, Andre, 24
Campeau, Pierre, 26
Cantelmy, Francois, 25
Capucine, Theodore, 26
Cardinal, Nicholas, heirs of, 18
Cardinal, Toussaint, 24
Cartier, --, 9
Cartier, P., 11
Cartier, Pierre, Junior, 25
Catt, P., 8
Catt, P., 19
Catt, Philip, 25
Caty, A., 2
Chabert, Pierre, 24
Chabotte, Joseph, Junior
Chapard, N., 6
Chapard, N., 8
Chapard, N., 13
Charbonneau, Germain, 24
Charbonneau, James, 4
Chartier, J., 19

Chartier, Michael, 26
Chartran, Jean Baptiste, 25
Chatignie, Ignace, 24
Cheroqui, Jean Baptiste, 26
Church wardens, 17
Claypole, Jeremiah, 1
Claypole, Jeremiah, 17
Clermont, Pierre, 25
Cloud, Joseph, 24
Coder, Andre, Junior, 24
Coder, Andre, Senior, 26
Coder, Henry, 26
Coder, Jean Baptiste, 25
Coder, Louis, 25
Coder, Pierre, 27
Coder, Toussaint, Junior, 25
Compagnotte, Pierre, 26
Conoyer, P., 18
Cornoyer, Alexis, 26
Coulter, Thomas, 7
Coulter, Thomas, 14
Courtois, Pierre, 26
Dace, Michael, 28
Dagenet, Ambroise, 27
Dagneau, --, 19
Danis, B., 7
Dapron, Joseph, 30
Dapron, Pierre, 30
Davis, J., 16
Davis, John, 23
Davis, John, 30
Day, Robert, 29
Decker, --, 5
Decker, Abraham, 25
Decker, Abraham, 29
Decker, Abraham, Junior, 24
Decker, Abraham, Junior, 29
Decker, Abraham, Senior, 21
Decker, Abraham, Senior, 28
Decker, Isaac, 16
Decker, Isaac, 29
Decker, Isaac, heirs of, 2
Decker, Isaac, heirs of, 3
Decker, Isaac, heirs of, 7
Decker, Isaac, heirs of, 12
Decker, Isaac, heirs of, 29
Decker, J., 1
Decker, John, 29
Decker, Joseph, Senior, 27

Decker, Luke, Esq., 2
Decker, Luke, Esq., 9
Decker, Luke, Esq., 12
Decker, Luke, Esq., 20
Decker, Luke, Esq., 29
Decker, Luke, Junior, 1
Decker, Luke, Junior, 16
Decker, Luke, 7
Decker, Luke, 27
Decker, M., 19
Decker, Moses, Senior, 27
Decker, Moses, 30
Decker, T., 27
Decker, Tobias, 29
Decoteau, --, 2
Deganne, Joseph, 30
Dejean, Philip, 27
Delaurier, John Baptiste, 5
Delaurier, S., 15
Delorie, Louis, 20
Deneau, Pierre, 28
Denoyon, L. T., 21
Denoyon, Louis Toussaint, 28
Denoyon, Louis, 28
Denoyon, Louis, 28
Depre, Francois, 30
Depron, Bernard, 27
Desbiens, Andre, 9
Devore, Philip, 28
Devore, P., 30
Devore, P., 30
Dielle, Charles, Junior, 29
Drouet, Antoine, dit Richardville, 15
Drouet, Antoine, dit Richardville, 18
Dubois, --, 12
Dubois, --, 18
Dubois, F., 10
Dubois, G. B., 3
Dubois, Jean Baptiste, 29
Dubois, Joseph, 28
Dubois, T., 13
Dubois, T., 18
Dubois, T., 20
Dubois, Toussaint, 1
Dubois, Toussaint, 2
Dubois, Toussaint, 2
Dubois, Toussaint, 6
Dubois, Toussaint, 8
Dubois, Toussaint, 9

Dubois, Toussaint, 9
Dubois, Toussaint, 9
Dubois, Toussaint, 12
Dubois, Toussaint, 14
Dubois, Toussaint, 15
Dubois, Toussaint, 17
Dubois, Toussaint, 22
Dubois, Toussaint, 22
Dubois, Toussaint, 22
Dubois, Toussaint, 22
Dubois, Toussaint, 27
Dubois, Toussaint, 28
Dubois, Toussaint, 28
Duchesne, Jean Baptiste, heirs of, 4
Dudevoir, C., 6
Dudevoir, Charles, dit Lachine, 29
Dumain, Jean Baptiste, 28
Dumais, Jacques, 28
Dumay, Francois, 27
Duquindre, Jean Baptiste, 28
Dutremble. See Jean Baptiste Lafleur
Edeline, Joseph, 30
Edeline, Nicholas, 30
Falls, Robert, 21
Faucher, Pierre, 31
Fidler, George, 14
Foreman, Joseph, 24
Foreman, Joseph, 31
Fortin, Jean Belony, 31
Frederick, Lewis, 30
Frederick, P., 5
Frederick, Peter, 31
Frederick, Sebastian, 30
Frederick, Sebastian, 30
Frichette, Jean Baptiste, 30
Gamelin, A., 8
Gamelin, Antoine, 8
Gamelin, Marguerite, heirs of, 11
Gamelin, Paul, heirs of, 11
Gibson, John, Senior, 29
Gilbeau. See Antoine Laframbois
Gilmore, Robert, 1
Gregoire, Joseph, 31
Grimarre, Pierre, 31
Guitarre, Jean Baptiste, 31
Haintonge. See St. Auge
Hamtramck, F., 7
Hamtramck, Jean F., heirs of, 18
Harbin, --, 1

Harbin, John, 11
Harbin, John, 25
Harbin, John, 28
Harbin, Joshua, heirs of, 6
Harness, Adam, 5
Harness, Adam, 8
Harness, Adam, 21
Harness, Adam, 24
Harness, Adam, 27
Harrison, William H., 6
Harrison, William H., 14
Harrison, William H., 17
Hazelton, Jarvis, 11
Hazleton, Daniel, 4
Hazleton, Jarvis, 21
Holder, Thomas, 25
Huff, Abraham, 8
Hunot, --, 12
Hunot, --, 18
Johnson, R., 1
Johnson, --, 23
Johnson, James, 26
Johnson, James, 27
Johnson, James, 29
Johnson, John, 27
Jones, John R., 4
Jones, John R., 10
Jones, J. R., 16
Jones, T., 1
Jones, Thomas, 24
Jones, Thomas, 27
Jordon, Ephraim, 27
Jordon, F., 27
Kirk, Henry, 24
Kirk, Henry, 30
Kuykindall, Abraham, 14
Kuykindall, Abraham, 21
Kuykindall, Abraham, 22
Kuykindall, Abraham, 28
Lachine. See Charles Dudevoir
Lacoste, Andre, 3
Lacroix, Jacques, 3
Lafevre, Pierre, 2
Lafleur, Jean Baptiste, dit Dutremble, 3
Laforest, Pierre, 1
Laforest, Pierre, 4
Laforest, P., 9
Laframbois, Antoine, dit Gilbeau, 1
Lalemier, Antoine, 8

Lalemier. See Antoine Petit
Lamotte, Josh., 12
Lamotte, Joseph, heirs of, 12
Langlois, Arne, 2
Languedoc, Andre, 1
Languedoc, Charles, 2
Languedoc, Charles, 3
Languedoc, Charles, 4
Languedoc, F., 2
Languedoc, Francois, 3
Larsh, Joseph, 1
Latrimouille, Jacques, 2
Latrimouille, Jacques, 2
Latrimouille, Jacques, 4
Latrimouille, Jacques, 4
Latrimouille, J., 4
Latrimouille, Jacques, 4
Ledgerwood, --, 5
Ledgerwood, James, 10
Ledgerwood, James, 11
Ledgerwood, James, 15
Ledgerwood, J., 16
Ledgerwood, --, 23
Ledgerwood, James, 25
Leech, Francois, 1
Leech, George, 1
Leech, George 1
Leech, --, 13
Lefevre, Antoine, 3
Lefevre, Antoine, 4
Lefevre, Antoine, 4
Lefevre, A., 11
Legarde, Jean Baptiste, 3
Legarde, Jean Baptiste, 3
Legrande, Jean M., 3
Legrande, Jean M., 4
Leveron, Joseph, 2
Leveron, Joseph, dit Meteye, 2
Leveron, Joseph, dit Meteye, 4
Levron, Louis, 7
Lindey, F., 30
Lindey, F., 30
Lionois, Jean Baptiste, and wife, 2
Lite, John, 4
Lognon, F., 5
Lognon, Joseph, 1
Mallett, Antoine, 5
Mallett, Francois, 5
Mallett, Francois, 6

Mallett, Francois
Mallett, Francois, heirs of, 6
Mallett, Francois, 6
Mallett, Francois, heirs of, 6
Mallett, Joseph, 6
Mallett, Louis, 6
Mallett, Pierre, 7
Marie, --, widow, 6
Marie, Antoine, 7
Marie, Antoine, 7
Marshal, Antoine, 8
Marshal, A., 11
Marshal, Antoine, 11
Marshal, John, 1
Martin, J. B., 2
Martin, John, 6
Martin, John, 7
Martin, John, 14
Martin, John, 21
Martin, J., 7
Martin, J., 9
Martin, William, 15
Matson, Ralph, 5
Mays, William, 5
Mays, Jeremiah, 5
Mays, J., 5
Mays, Robert, 6
Mays, R., 19
McClure, J., 4
McGowen, William, 3
McIntosh, William, 7
McIntosh, William, 9
McIntosh, William, 12
McIntosh, William, 15
McIntosh, William, 18
McIntosh, William, 22
McIntosh, William, 25
McIntosh, William, 30
McNulty, James, 7
Mehl, Frederick, 5
Meteye, Louis, 7
Meteye. See Joseph Leveron
Meuville, Joseph, 5
Millett, Jean Baptiste, 7
Mills, John, heirs of, 4
Mills, John, heirs of, 22
Mills, John, heirs of, 26
Mills, John, heirs of, 29
Mills, John, heirs of, 30

Mills, Zachariah, 26
Mills, Zachariah, 30

Minor, Isaac, 3
Minor, Isaac, 13
Montplaisir, Andre, 2
Montplaisir, Andre, 6
Morrison, W., 6
Morrison, William, 13
Morrison, William, 25
Murphy, John, 5
Noye, Jacob, 7
Noye, Jacob, heirs of, 7
Ockletree, J., 4
Ockletree, John, 14
Ockletree, John, 25
Ouilette, Jean Baptiste, 8
Page, G., 7
Page, Guillaume, 8
Page, Guillaume, 9
Page, Guillaume, 10
Page, Joseph, 10
Page, William, 10
Page, William, 11
Paine, Louis, 10
Pancake, Joseph, 8
Pappino, Peter, 9
Parent, Joachim, 9
Park, William, 11
Pea, D., 27
Pea, Daniel, 8
Pea, Henry, 23
Pea, Henry, 26
Pea, Jacob, 8
Pea, John, 8
Pea, John, 10
Pea, J., 19
Pea, --, 19
Pea, John, 22
Pearou, Amable, 10
Pedoret, Joseph, Junior, 10
Peltier, Andrew, 8
Peltier, Eustace, 9
Perron, Pierre, 9
Perron, Pierre, 9
Perron, Jean Baptiste, 9
Perrot, Nicholas, 10
Petit, Antoine, dit Lalemier, 8
Petit, Antoine, dit Lalemier, 8

Petit, A., 9
Petit, A., 12
Pfannkuchen. See Pancake (translation)
Pillars, Richard, 9
Plough, J., 21
Pluchon, Louis, 9
Price, B. D., 8
Price, Benjamin D., 16
Price, B. D., 20
Purcell, Edward, 13
Querre, --, 15
Querrie, --, 9
Querrie, Pierre, 11
Querrie, Pierre, 11
Racine St. Marie, Francois, 12
Racine, --, 1
Racine, --, 4
Racine, A., 12
Racine, Angelique, 13
Racine, Francois, 12
Racine, Francois, 13
Racine, Jean Baptiste, 11
Racine, Jean Baptiste, 12
Racine, Jean Baptiste, 12
Ramsay, Allen, 12
Ramsay, A., 27
Ravalet, Jean Baptiste, 13
Ravalet, Louis, 13
Reed, William, 5
Reed, William, 5
Reed, William, 14
Reed, --, 19
Reeves, Abner, heirs of, 8
Reeves, A., 13
Richard, Marie, 11
Richard, Marie, 11
Richard, Marie, 12
Richard, --, dit Antaya, widow, 13
Richardville, --, 11
Richardville. See Antoine Drouet
Rivet, J. F., 9
Robb, David, 23
Robb, David, 25
Robb, James, 28
Robbins, John, 11
Robbins, John, heirs of, 11
Robbins, John, 28
Robins, Julia, 19
Robinson, Andrew, 13

Roy, Andre, 13
Saint Dezier. See St. Dezier
Saint Aubin. See St. Aubin
Saint Auge. See St. Auge
Saint Marie. See St. Marie
Savage, John, 14
Seguin, Alexis, 14
Selby, Thomas, 14
Sevans, Ebenezer, 31
Simpson, P., 7
Simpson, Patrick, 12
Simpson, Patrick, 14
Simpson, P., 26
Slaughter, Lawrence, 14
Small, John, 14
Small, Thomas, 15
Smith, Daniel, 5
Smith, D., 10
Smith, Daniel, 13
Smith, Daniel, 13
Smith, Daniel, 21
Smith, Daniel, 27
Snapp, A. F., 8
Snapp, A. F., 8
Snapp, Abraham F., 11
Snapp, Abraham F., 11
Snapp, Abraham F., 13
Snapp, Abraham F., 14
Snapp, Abraham F., 16
Snapp, Abraham F., 28
Souci, --, 15
Spears, Noah, 21
Spears, Noah, 24
Spears, Noah, 27
Spech, Henry, 13
St. Dezier, --, heirs of, 13
St. Aubin, Joseph, 14
St. Marie, Etienne, 15
St. Aubin, Jean Baptiste, 15
St. Marie, Francois, 15
St. Auge, Joseph, dit Haintonge, 15
Stepp, Abraham, 26
Stepp, Abraham, 26
Stilwell, John, 20
Stilwell, John, 31
Sullivan, Daniel, 15
Sullivan, Susan, 7
Sullivan, Susan, 9
Sullivan, Susan, 10

Sullivan, Susan, 15
Tevebaugh, Jacob, Junior, 16
Tevebaugh, Jacob, Junior, heirs of, 16
Tevebaugh, Jacob, 31
Thomas, Jesse, 21
Thorn, Charles, 15
Thorn, Charles, 16
Thorn, Charles, 16
Thorn, Daniel, 16
Thorn, Jacob, 16
Thorn, Jacob, 16
Thorn, Michael, Senior, 16
Thorn, Michael, Junior, 16
Thorn, Michael, 16
Thorn, Peter, 16
Tougas, J., 7
Tougas, J., 14
Tougas, Joseph, 16
Tougas, Joseph, 17
United States Garrison, 12
Vachette, Pierre A., 19
Valli, Alexander, 17
Valli, Alexander, 17
Valli, Alexander, 17
Valli, Alexander, 17
Valli, Alexander, 18
Valli, Alexander, 19
Valli, Alexander, Junior, 19
Vanderburgh, Henry, 3
Vanderburgh, Henry, 15
Vanderburgh, Henry, 15
Vanderburgh, Henry, 26
Vanderburgh, Henry, 26
Vanderburgh, Henry, 29
Vanderburgh, John, 31
Vaudry, J. B., 4
Vaudry, Jean Baptiste, widow of, 17
Vaudry, Jean Baptiste, 18
Vaudry, Jean Baptiste, 18
Vaudry, Jean Baptiste, 19
Vaudry, Jean Baptiste, 19
Vigo, F., 1
Vigo, Francis, 3
Vigo, Francis, 4
Vigo, Francis, 4
Vigo, Francis, 4
Vigo, Francis, 10
Vigo, Francis, 10
Vigo, Francis, 10

Vigo, --, 12
Vigo, Francis, 17
Vigo, Francis, 17
Vigo, Francis, 18
Vigo, Francis, 18
Vigo, Francis, 18
Vigo, Francis, 19
Vigo, Francis, 23
Villeneuve, --, 7
Villeneuve, Charles, 17
Villeneuve, Charles, 18
Villeneuve, --, 19
Villeray, Jean Baptiste, 18
Vincennes church, 17
Wallace, George, Junior, 18
Warth, Robert, 28
Watkins, Samuel, 20
Westfall, Abraham, 3
Westfall, A., 16
Westfall, Abraham, 19
Westfall, A., 19
Westfall, John, 20
White, Isaac, 13
Widner, John, 19
Widner, John, 19
Wilkins, Andrew, 19
Wilkins, A., 19
Williams, Francis, 25
Wilmore, John, 11
Wilmore, John, 19
Wilmore, John, 20
Wilson, --, widow, 5
Wilson, Alexander, 19
Wilson, Alexander, heirs of, 19
Wilson, J., 19
Wilson, Alexander, 19
Wilson, Alexander, heirs of, 19
Wilson, Francis, 20
Wilson, W., 22
Wyant, C., 3
Wyant, Christopher, 7
Wyant, Christopher, 13
Wyant, Christopher, 20
Wyant, Christopher, 20
Wyant, --, 23
Wyant, Christopher, 23

Selections from **The American State Papers**, No. 4

French and British Land Grants in the

Post Vincennes (Indiana) District

1750-1784
(Continued)

Clifford Neal Smith

First printing, September 1996   rz
Reprint, November 1996   qz

FOREWORD

The American State Papers are official public documents printed privately long before the Congressional Printing Office existed. The printing of public documents during the very early Congresses was done without any general provision of law as to what should be printed. Even as early as 1829 the clerk of the House of Representatives reported that, for the period 1793-1803 not a vestige of manuscript and only a scattered few printed copies were extant. A contributing factor was the destruction of the Capitol building in 1814 by fire.

In 1821 a bill was passed which authorized the publication of 750 copies of all the documents that could be found. The documents were published by two private companies: Gales and Seaton, and Duff Green. Of the two publications, Gales and Seaton is the larger. The Duff Green collection of documents are less comprehensive than the Gales and Seaton collection, and there are many differences in the pagination, particularly in later volumes.

Both publishers appear to have divided the original documents into general subject categories: Foreign Affairs, Indian Affairs, Finance, Commerce and Navigation, Military Affairs, Naval Affairs, Post Office Department, Public Land, and Claim. For genealogical and family history researchers, the last two categories--Public Land and Claims--are the most valuable, and it is from these two categories that this monograph *Selections from **The American State Papers*** will be made. The Public Land category, in eight volumes, covers the period 1789-1837; the Claims category, in one volume, covers the period 1790-1823.

In 1972 an attempt was made to index all names in the Public Land and Claims categories of the American State Papers; the index, although monumental, is, however, not complete. All researchers are urged to read pages i through xxvii of

Phillip McMullin, editor, *Grassroots of America: A Computerized Index to the American State Papers: Land Grants and Claims (1789-1837) with Other Aids to Research* (Salt Lake City, Utah: Gendex Corporation, 1972).

The present *Selections from the American State Papers* are the selections, by narrower subject matter, from the Gales and Seaton edition, made by this compiler for the use of genealogists and family historians because the original volumes are now very rare and, no doubt, inaccessible to most researchers.

(ASP 8:1:570)

List of Lands confirmed by the different
Governors in virtue of Militia rights--continued
Those with a number affixed are surveyed in a body
on the southeast side of White river.

Claimants:
 Original: **Goyeau, Antoine**
 Present: **James Johnson, Esq.**
Tract 96. On White river, joining **B. Beckes, John Martin**, and **James Johnson.**

Claimants:
 Original: **Garzee** or **Carzee, Jean**
 Present: **John Mills,** heirs of
Tract 100.

Claimants:
 Original: **Guiyeau, Pierre,** heirs of
 Present: **Walker Reed**
--, surveyed; on White river, joining **B. Beckes, J[ohn] Martin,** and **James Johnson.**

Claimants:
 Original: **Grimarre, Jean Baptiste**
 Present: **Henry Vanderburgh**
Tract 15.

Claimants:
 Original: **Gracoit** or **Gracet, John**
 Present: **Peter Lismain**
Not surveyed.

Claimants:
 Original: **Harbin, John**
 Present: **Henry Pea**
--, surveyed; on north side of White river.

Claimants:
 Original: **Harbin, Joshua**
 Present: **Joshua Harbin,** heirs of
-- surveyed; on White river, at the ferry.

Claimants:
  Original: **Hunot, Joseph, Junior**
  Present: **Francis Anthis** and **Samuel Baird**
 --, surveyed; on north side of White river, joining **Joseph Decker**, **A. Ramsay**, and **D. Crock**.

Claimants:
  Original: **Hunot, Gabriel**
  Present: **Philip Catt**
 --, surveyed; on river Des Chis, joining said Catt, **B. Beckes**, and **A. Decker**.

Claimants:
  Original: **Harpin, Amable**
  Present: **Henry Vanderburgh**
Tract 16.

Claimants:
  Original: **Holliday, Ezekiel**
  Present: not entered
Tract 113.

Claimants:
  Original: **Hunot, Antoine**, heirs of
  Present: **John Bailey**
Not surveyed.

Claimants:
  Original: **Hamelin, Francois**
  Present: not entered

Claimants:
  Original: **Johnson, James** (turner)
  Present: **James Johnson**
 --, surveyed; near White river, bounded by **John Crawford**, **Isaac Baker**, and **E. Biddle**.

Claimants:
  Original: **Johnson, James, Esq.**
  Present: **James Black**
 --, surveyed; between Bosseron and Marie creeks, joining **F. Williams** and **F. Berger**.

Claimants:
 Original: **Jordon, Thomas**
 Present: **Thomas Jordon**
 --, surveyed; on waters of White river, bounded by **W. Mayes, M. Decker**, and **E. Biddle**.

Claimants:
 Original: **Johnston, Robert**
 Present: **John Durham**
 --, surveyed; on Marie creek, joining the donation tract.

Claimants:
 Original: **Jones, John R.**
 Present: **Toussaint Dubois**
 Tract 28.

Claimants:
 Original: **Johnson, John, Junior**
 Present: **John Gibson**
 Tract 98.

Claimants:
 Original: **Joyeuse, Joseph**
 Present: **Henry Vanderburgh**
 Tract 13.

Claimants:
 Original: **Johnson, Richard**
 Present: **John Johnson**
 Tract 99.

Claimants:
 Original: **Latour, Pierre**
 Present: **Noah Spears**
 Tract 46.

Claimants:
 Original: **Lefevre, Antoine**
 Present: **John Mills**, heirs of, and **A. Pea**
 Tract 36.

Claimants:
 Original: **Lapointe, Joseph, dit Orleans**
 Present: **Thomas Jones**
 Tract 71.

Claimants:
 Original: **Laforest, Pierre**
 Present: **Keen Fields**
 Tract 11.

Claimants:
 Original: **Labuxierre, Louis**
 Present: **Samuel McClure**
 --, surveyed; on waters of Marie creek, joining **John Small**.

Claimants:
 Original: **Legrand, Joseph**
 Present: **Joshua Harbin**, heirs of
 --, surveyed; on river Des Chis.

Claimants:
 Original: **Letemps, Jean Baptiste**
 Present: **Toussaint Dubois**
 Tract 52.

Claimants:
 Original: **Lindey, Frederick**
 Present: **Toussaint Dubois**
 Tract 57.

Claimants:
 Original: **Lefeuillade*, Francois**
 Present: **John Gibson**
 --, surveyed; on waters of Mill creek, joining **James Johnson**.
 [*so spelled]

Claimants:
 Original: **Legrand, Jean M.**
 Present: **William McIntosh**
 Tract 63.

Claimants:
 Original: **Lafeuillade*, Pierre**
 Present: **Henry Vanderburgh**
 Tract 5. [*so spelled]

Claimants:
 Original: **Langlois, Francois**
 Present: **Zachariah Mills**
 Tract 114.

Claimants:
 Original: **Legarde, Jean**
 Present: **Zachariah Mills**
 Tract 115.

Claimants:
 Original: **Loneveu, Louis**
 Present: **Robert Buntin**
 --, surveyed; on Mill creek, joining the donation tract.

Claimants:
 Original: **Legrand, Jean Baptiste**
 Present: **William Wells**
 Tract 23.

Claimants:
 Original: **Lardoise, Amable, Junior**
 Present: **Francis Vigo**
 --, surveyed; on Mill creek, joining **P. Simpson** and heirs of **F. Cornoyer**.

Claimants:
 Original: **Lee, William**
 Present: **James Ledgerwood**
 --, surveyed; on waters of Bosseron creek, joining **Thomas Holder**.

Claimants:
 Original: **Lamotte, Joseph**
 Present: **Abraham Barrackman**
 --, surveyed.

Claimants:
 Original: **Lafontaine, Etienne**
 Present: **Abraham T. Snapp**
 Tract 7.

Claimants:
 Original: **Lafleur, Joseph, dit Perodo**
 Present: **Daniel Pea**
 Tract 6.

Claimants:
 Original: **Lecoteau**, or **Decoteau, Joseph**
 Present: **Henry Vanderburgh**
 Tract 44.

Claimants:
 Original: **Lafferty, John**
 Present: **William Morrison**, heirs of
 --, surveyed; on the north side of White river, joining other lands of said Morrison.

Claimants:
 Original: **Laderoute, Jacques**
 Present: not entered
 Tract 9.

Claimants:
 Original: **Laforest, Louis**
 Present: not entered
 Tract 111.

Claimants:
 Original: **Lafeuillade, Jean Baptiste**
 Present: not entered
 Tract 80.

(ASP 8:1:571)

Claimants:
 Original: **Lowe, John**
 Present: not entered
 Tract 22.

Claimants:
 Original: **Lalumier, Antoine, dit Petit**
 Present: **Luke Decker, Esq.**
 --, surveyed; on the north side of White river, joining **Tobias Decker**.

Claimants:
 Original: **Lefevre, Louis**
 Present: not entered
 Tract 78.

Claimants:
 Original: **Menard, Pierre**
 Present: **Adam Harness**
 --, surveyed; on white river, bounded by **J. Decker**, **T. Decker**, and **A. Ramsay**.

Claimants:
 Original: **Murphey, John**
 Present: **Daniel Smith**
 Tract 85.

Claimants:
 Original: **Mette, Rene**
 Present: **Joseph Foreman**
 Tract 41.

Claimants:
 Original: **Martin, John**
 Present: **John Martin**
 --, surveyed; near White river, joining his other surveys.

Claimants:
 Original: **Martin, Alexander**
 Present: 50 acres, **Alexander Martin**, heirs of
 --, surveyed; on waters of White river, bounded by said Martin, **F. Biddle**, and **J. Thomas**

Claimants:
 Original: **Martin, Alexander**
 Present: 50 acres, **William McGowen**
 --, surveyed; in the barrens, joining his 50 survey.

Claimants:
 Original: **Mayes, William**
 Present: **William Mayes**
 --, surveyed; between Des Chis and White rivers, joining **Robert Mayes**.

Claimants:
 Original: **Mayes, Jeremiah**
 Present: **Jeremiah Mayes**
 --, surveyed; between Des Chs and White rivers, joining Matson's station.

Claimants:
 Original: **Moyse, Charles**
 Present: **John Reel**
 Tract 14.

Claimants:
 Original: **Matson, Ralph**
 Present: **William Watson**
 --, surveyed; on Marie creek, bounded by **Joseph Black**, **Thomas Anderson**, and **F. Berger**.

Claimants:
 Original: **Melloche, Antoine**
 Present: **James Johnson, Esq.**
 Tract 97.

Claimants:
 Original: **McIntosh, William**
 Present: **William McIntosh**
 Tract 66.

Claimants:
 Original: **Mette, Joseph**
 Present: **Henry Pea**
 Tract 72.

Claimants:
 Original: **Meredy, Daniel**
 Present: **J. Mills**, heirs of, 50 [acres] and **R. Falls** 50 [acres].

Claimants:
 Original: **Martin, Jean Baptiste**
 Present: **Henry Vanderburgh**
 Tract 1.

Claimants:
 Original: **Maisonville, Joseph, Junior**
 Present: not entered
 Tract 65.

Claimants:
 Original: **Maisonville, Jean Baptiste**
 Present: not entered
 Tract 59.

Claimants:
 Original: **Monviel, Joseph**
 Present: not entered
 Tract 33.

Claimants:
 Original: **Midler, Frederick**
 Present: not entered
 Tract 108.

Claimants:
 Original: **Ouellette, Alexis**
 Present: not entered
 Tract 18.

Claimants:
 Original: **Pea, John**
 Present: **John Pea**
 --, surveyed; on the waters of river Des Chis, bounded by **William Reed, J. Pea,** and vacant lands.

Claimants:
 Original: **Pea, Jacob**
 Present: **John Pea,** heirs of
 --, surveyed; on White river, bounded by **D. Pea** and bottoms of said river.

Claimants:
 Original: **Pea, Daniel**
 Present: **Elias Biddle**
 --, surveyed; on waters of White river, joining **Thomas Jordon** and said Biddle.

Claimants:
 Original: **Peters, Godfrey**
 Present: **William Morrison,** heirs of
 Tract 90.

Claimants:
 Original: **Page, Joseph**
 Present: **Nicholas Egbert**
 Tract 3.

Claimants:
 Original: **Poirier, Francois**
 Present: **Henry Vanderburgh**
 Tract 4.

Claimants:
 Original: **Potdivin, Jean Baptiste**
 Present: **Robert Buntin**
 --, surveyed; on Mill creek, joining the donation tract.

Claimants:
 Original: **Potdivin, Joseph**
 Present: **Robert Buntin**
 --, surveyed; on Mill creek, joining the donation tract.

Claimants:
 Original: **Potdivin, Francois, dit Arpin**
 Present: **William Wells**
 Tract 21.

Claimants:
 Original: **Preville, Louis**
 Present: **Abraham Snapp**
 Tract 81.

Claimants:
 Original: **Pea, Henry**
 Present: **Henry Pea**
 --, surveyed; on Mill creek, joining **John Harbin,** and other lands of said Pea.

Claimants:
 Original: **Poirier, Pierre, dit Desloges**
 Present: **James Ledgerwood**
 --, surveyed; on Bosseron creek.

Claimants:
 Original: **Querre, Pierre, Junior**
 Present: **Jeremiah Claypole**
 --, not surveyed.

Claimants:
 Original: **Ruyard, Joseph**
 Present: **Jacob Tevebaugh**
 Tract 68.

Claimants:
 Original: **Robbins, John**
 Present: **John Robbins,** heirs of
 --, surveyed.

Claimants:
 Original: **Riend, Joseph**
 Present: **Robert Hyneman**
 Tract 70.

Claimants:
 Original: **Robert, Pierre**
 Present: **Toussaint Dubois**
 Tract 55.

Claimants:
 Original: **Rimbault, Henry**
 Present: **William McIntosh**
 Tract 48.

Claimants:
 Original: **Roderigue, Diego**
 Present: **Samuel Baird**
 Tract 87.

Claimants:
 Original: **Ramsay, Allen**
 Present: **Robert Buntin**
 --, surveyed; on Mill creek, joining the donation tract.

Claimants:
 Original: **Smith, Daniel**
 Present: **Daniel Smith**
 Tract 86.

Claimants:
 Original: **Smith, William**
 Present: **William Smith**, heirs of
 Tract 88.

Claimants:
 Original: **St. Louis, Jean, dit Ditard**
 Present: **Joseph Foreman**
 Tract 42.

Claimants:
 Original: **Smith, William T.**
 Present: **John Reed**
 Tract 19.

Claimants:
 Original: **Snapp, Abraham F.**
 Present: **Abraham F. Snapp**
 --, surveyed; on Small's creek, joining **John Purcell**, and low lands of Wabash.

Claimants:
 Original: **Small, Thomas**
 Present: **Abraham F. Snapp**
 -- surveyed; on Small's creek.

Claimants:
 Original: **St. Aubin, Louis**
 Present: **William Johnson**
 Tract 6.

Claimants:
 Original: **Simpson, Patrick**
 Present: **Patrick Simpson**
 --, surveyed; on waters of Mill creek, joining **R. Buntin, F. Vigo,** vacant lands, and other lands of said Simpson.

Claimants:
 Original: **Severe, Louis**
 Present: **John Mills**, heirs of
 Tract 101.

(ASP 8:1:572)

Claimants:
 Original: **Soulier, Jean Louis**
 Present: **William McIntosh**
 Tract 10.

Claimants:
 Original: **Simarre, Francois**
 Present: **Henry Vanderburgh**
 Tract 106.

Claimants:
 Original: **Smith, Anthony**
 Present: **Robert Buntin**
 --, surveyed; on Mill creek, joining the donation tract.

Claimants:
 Original: **Shoebrooks, Edward**
 Present: **John Mills**, heirs of
 Tract 112.

Claimants:
 Original: **Store, Frederick**
 Present: not entered
 Tract 94.

Claimants:
 Original: **Stokely, Francis**
 Present: not entered
 Tract 69.

Claimants:
 Original: **St. Marie, Andre**
 Present: not entered
 Tract 2.

Claimants:
 Original: **Thorn, Jacob**
 Present: **Frederick Mehl**
 --, surveyed; on east boundary of the commons, by F. Mehl.

Claimants:
 Original: **Thorn, Charles**
 Present: **Daniel Smith**
 Tract 91.

Claimants:
 Original: **Thorn, Michael**
 Present: **Isaac Baker**
 --, surveyed; on White river, bounded by **W. Mayes** and **James Johnson**.

Claimants:
 Original: **Thorn, Michael, Junior**
 Present: **Michael Thorn, Junior**
 --, surveyed; on north branch of river Des Chis, bounded by said Thorn and **J. R. Jones**.

Claimants:
 Original: **Theil, Isaac**
 Present: **John Harbin**
 --, surveyed; on river Des Chis, bounded by other lands of said Harbin.

Claimants:
 Original: **Thorn, Daniel**
 Present: **Francis Anthis**
 --, surveyed; on north side White river, joining **A. Ramsay, D. Crock,** and **Jos[eph] Decker**.

Claimants:
 Original: **Tougas, Auguste**
 Present: **Ursule** and **Julie Bosseron**
 --, surveyed; on north side Wabash, joining Bosseron.

Claimants:
 Original: **Thorn, Peter**
 Present: **John Johnson**
 Tract 95.

14

Claimants:
Original: **Tougas, Joseph, Junior**
Present: **Robert Buntin**
--, surveyed; on waters of Mill creek, joining **P. Barrackman** and **Fred[erick] Berger**.

Claimants:
Original: **Tessier, Francois**
Present: **William Wells**
Tract 20.

Claimants:
Original: **Tougas, William**
Present: **James Ledgerwood**
--, surveyed; on Bosseron [creek], joining other lands of said Ledgerwood.

Claimants:
Original: **Thorn, Solomon**
Present: **Michael Thorn**
--, surveyed; on north branch of river Des Chis, joining his own militia survey.

Claimants:
Original: **Villeneuve, Charles**
Present: **Toussaint Dubois**
Tract 109.

Claimants:
Original: **Vanderburgh, Henry**
Present: **Isaac Decker**, heirs of
-- surveyed; on north side White river, near Decker's station.

Claimants:
Original: **Valcour, Jean Baptiste**
Present: **Henry Vanderburgh**
Tract 126.

Claimants:
Original: **Westfall, John N.**
Present: **Joshua Harbin**, heirs of
-- surveyed; on waters of river Des Chis, joining other lands of said Harbin.

Claimants:
Original: **Westfall, Abraham**
Present: **Abraham Westfall**
--, surveyed; on waters of river Des Chis, joining **Michael Thorn** and others.

Claimants:
 Original: **Wilmore, John**
 Present: **John Davis**
 --, surveyed; on Bosseron [creek], joining -- **Ledgerwood**, and other lands of said Davis.

Claimants:
 Original: **Wyant, Christopher**
 Present: **Christopher Wyant**
 --, surveyed; on waters of Little river, joining said Wyant.

Claimants:
 Original: **Wilson, Isaac**
 Present: **Isaac Wilson**
 --, surveyed; on the south side of White river, bounded by **P. Catt, J. Pea**, and heirs of **A. Wilson**.

(ASP 8:1:573)

Supplement to Document D
List of Lands confirmed by the Commissioners in virtue of
French or British grants, and of court and commandant deeds

Claimants:
 Original: **Boucher, Vital**
 Present: **Vital Boucher**
 Acreage: 50
 Appropriated; within the tract appropriated for the donation to the heads of families.

Claimants:
 Original: **Bordeleau, Antoine**
 Present: **Antoine Bordeleau**, heirs of
 Acreage: 136
 Not appropriated; at the little village on the northwest side of the Wabash.

Claimants:
 Original: **Baker, Joel**
 Present: **John Edgar**
 Acreage: 400
 Appropriated; on waters of Marie creek, joining **Thomas Small**, within the donation tract.

Claimants:
 Original: **Brouillet, Francis**
 Present: **William H. Harrison**
 Acreage: 68
 Not appropriated; on the northwest side of the Wabash, a little above the town of Vincennes.

Claimants:
 Original: **Conger, Jonathan**
 Present: **Jonathan Conger**
 Acreage: 400
 Not appropriated; on the south side, and opposite the forks of White river.

Claimants:
 Original: **Compagnotte, Francis**
 Present: **Francis Compagnotte**
 Acreage: 136
 Not appropriated; below the lower prairie.

Claimants:
 Original: **Danis, Honori***
 Present: **Jeremiah Claypole**, as heirs of Danis
 Acreage: 50
 Appropriated; within the donation tract. [*so spelled]

Claimants:
 Original: **Duchesne, Jean Baptiste**
 Present: **William H. Harrison**
 Acreage: 68
 Not appropriated; in the upper prairie, joining on both sides lands late of -- **Lachine** and -- **Cardinal**.

Claimants:
 Original: **Dumay, --**
 Present: Heirs of -- **Dumay**
 Acreage: 170
 Not appropriated; on the northwest side of the Wabash, opposite the town of Vincennes.

Claimants:
 Original: **Delaurier, Jean Baptiste**
 Present: **Jean Baptiste Delaurier**
 Acreage: 102
 Not appropriated; below Cathelinette prairie.

Claimants:
 Original: **Dubois, Jean Baptiste**
 Present: **Robert Buntin**
 Acreage: 300
 Not appropriated; in the forks of Marie creek.

Claimants:
 Original: **Gamelin, Antoine**
 Present: **Antoine Gamelin**, widow & heirs of
 Acreage: 50
 Not appropriated; below the Manimelles, on the southeast of the Wabash.

Claimants:
 Original: **Glaze, Adam**
 Present: **Adam Glaze**
 Acreage: 100
 Appropriated; within the donation tract.

Claimants:
 Original: **Harpier, Jean Baptiste**
 Present: **George Catt**
 Acreage: 68
 Not appropriated; on the river Des Chis, joining other lands of Catt.

Claimants:
 Original: **Howell, John**
 Present: **John Howell**, heirs and assignees of
 Acreage: 136
 Not appropriated; below and joining **John Small**, on the north side of the Wabash.

Claimants:
 Original: **Levron, Louis, dit Meteye**
 Present: **Louis Levron**, heirs of
 Acreage: 50
 Appropriated; within the donation tract.

Claimants:
 Original: **Languedoc, Francis**
 Present: **Robert Buntin**
 Acreage: 400
 Appropriated; on the waters of Mill creek.

Claimants:
 Original: **Leproux, Joseph**
 Present: **Jean Baptiste Delaurier**
 Acreage: 68
 Not appropriated; in the Cathelinette prairie.

Claimants:
 Original: **Laforest, Pierre**
 Present: **John Marshall**
 Acreage: 136
 Not appropriated; river Des Chis prairie, near Decker's station.

Claimants:
 Original: **Languedoc, Andre**
 Present: **Benjamin Reed**, heirs of
 Acreage: 340
 Appropriated; within the donation on Mill creek.

Claimants:
 Original: **Languedoc, Andre**
 Present: **William Reed**
 Acreage: 200
 Not appropriated; on the southeast of Vincennes, back of the first concession, called the brick yard.

Claimants:
 Original: **Levins, Nicholas**
 Present: **Elias Biddle**
 Acreage: 200
 Appropriated; on White river.

Claimants:
 Original: **Lindey, Frederick**
 Present: **Frederick Lindey**
 Acreage: 200
 Appropriated; within the donation.

Claimants:
 Original: **Lefleur, --**
 Present: **Daniel Sullivan**, heirs of
 Acreage: 136
 Not appropriated; on the river Des Chis prairie.

Claimants:
 Original: **Mulliken, James**
 Present: **James Mulliken**, heirs of
 Acreage: 400
 Appropriated; on the waters of White river, within the donation.

Claimants:
 Original: **Marie, Antoine**
 Present: **Antoine Marie,** heirs of
 Acreage: 272
Appropriated; on Marie creek, at a place called the Cap.

Claimants:
 Original: **Morin, De Valcour, Francis**
 Present: **Francis M. De Valcour**
 Acreage: 50
Appropriated; on land now owned by **James Johnson, Esq.**, on Mill Creek.

Claimants:
 Original: **Pettier, Marie J.**
 Present: **Pierre Querre** and wife
 Acreage: 204
Appropriated; on Mill creek.

Claimants:
 Original: **Pea, Jacob, Junior**
 Present: **Jacob Pea, Junior**
 Acreage: 100
Appropriated; on head waters of Wilson's creek, within the donation tract.

Claimants:
 Original: **Ravalet, Louis**
 Present: **Louis Ravalet**
 Acreage: 136
Not appropriated; on Raccoon creek, northwest side of Wabash.

Claimants:
 Original: **Raux, --**
 Present: **Jean Baptiste Laplante**
 Acreage: 59.80
Not appropriated; on northwest side of the Wabash a little above Vincennes.

Claimants:
 Original: **Racine, Andrew, dit St. Marie**
 Present: **Andrew Racine, dit St. Marie**
 Acreage: 136
Not appropriated; on the northwest side of the Wabash, a little above Vincennes.

Claimants:
 Original: **Racine, Jean Baptiste**
 Present: **Jean Baptiste Racine,** heirs of
 Acreage: 272
Not appropriated; near Faux Chenal, joining **F. Mallett**'s heirs.

Claimants:
 Original: **Sentier, Olivier**
 Present: **Jean Baptiste Delaurier** and wife
 Acreage: 50
Appropriated; on the waters of the river Des Chis, on the island road.

Claimants:
 Original: **Tougas, Jean Baptiste**
 Present: **Jean Baptiste Tougas,** heirs of
 Acreage: 204
Not appropriated; on the northwest side of Wabash, opposite Vincennes.

(ASP 8:1:574)

Supplement D--Continued
List of Lands confirmed by the Commissioners
in virtue of Militia rights

Claimants:
 Original: **Culbert, John**
 Present: **John Culbert,** or heirs of
 Acreage: 100

Claimants:
 Original: **Dempsey, Hugh**
 Present: **Hugh Dempsey**
 Acreage: 100

Claimants:
 Original: **Dobbins, Matthew**
 Present: **Matthew Dobbins,** or heirs of
 Acreage: 100

Claimants:
 Original: **Foizy, Francois**
 Present: **Samuel Baird**
 Acreage: 100

Claimants:
  Original: **Goder, Rene**
  Present: **Rene Goder**
  Acreage: 100

Claimants:
  Original: **Jordon, Ephraim**
  Present: **Ephraim Jordon**
  Acreage: 100

Claimants:
  Original: **Moore, Samuel**
  Present: **Abraham F. Snapp**
  Acreage: 100

Claimants:
  Original: **Mays, Robert**
  Present: **Robert Mays**, or heirs of
  Acreage: 100

Claimants:
  Original: **Pacquin, Francis**
  Present: **Francis Pacquin**
  Acreage: 100

Claimants:
  Original: **Pea, Abraham**
  Present: **Abraham Pea**
  Acreage: 100

Claimants:
  Original: **Savage, John**
  Present: **John Savage**, heirs of
  Acreage: 100

Claimants:
  Original: **Small, John**
  Present: **John Small**
  Acreage: 100

Claimants:
  Original: **Sampson, Alexander**
  Present: **Alexander Sampson**
  Acreage: 100

Claimants:
  Original: **Watts, James**
  Present: **James Watts**, heirs of
  Acreage: 100

(ASP 8:1:574)
List of Donation rights
confirmed by the Commissioners

Claimants:
 Original: **Boucher, Charles**
 Present: **Charles Boucher,** heirs of
 Acreage: 400

Claimants:
 Original: **Bolon, Hyppolite**
 Present: **Hyppolite Bolon**
 Acreage: 400

Claimants:
 Original: **Becquet, --,** widow of
 Present: **Samuel Baird**
 Acreage: 400

Claimants:
 Original: **Brossard, Joseph**
 Present: **Joseph Brossard,** heirs or assigns of
 Acreage: 400

Claimants:
 Original: **Conteaux, Jacques**
 Present: **Jacques Conteaux,** heirs or assigns of
 Acreage: 400

Claimants:
 Original: **Crepeau, Louis**
 Present: **Louis Crepeau,** heirs of
 Acreage: 400

Claimants:
 Original: **Cantelmy, Francis**
 Present: **Laurent Bazadone**
 Acreage: 300

Claimants:
 Original: **Clermont, Lizette**
 Present: **Lizette Clermont,** heirs of
 Acreage: 400

Claimants:
 Original: **Cardinal, Marianne W.**
 Present: **Cardinal, --,** widow, her heirs or assigns
 Acreage: 400

Claimants:
 Original: **Clermont, Michael**
 Present: **John Daly**
 Acreage: 400

Claimants:
 Original: **Dagenat, Ambroise**
 Present: **Ambroise Dagenat,** heirs of
 Acreage: 400

Claimants:
 Original: **Grimarre, Pierre, Senior**
 Present: **Pierre Grimarre, Senior,** heirs of
 Acreage: 400

Claimants:
 Original: **Goder, Pierre**
 Present: **Pierre Goder,**
 Acreage: 400

Claimants:
 Original: **Morin, Francis, dit De Valcour**
 Present: **Francis Morin De Valcour**
 Acreage: 400

Claimants:
 Original: **Perron, Pierre, Junior**
 Present: **Pierre Perron,** heirs of
 Acreage: 400

Claimants:
 Original: **Pettier, Andrew**
 Present: **Andrew Pettier,** heirs of
 Acreage: 400

Claimants:
 Original: **Thiriot, Jean C.,** widow of
 Present: **Julie Thiriot**
 Acreage: 400

(ASP 8:1:574)
Confirmations made since our
report of March 25, 1806

Claimants:
 Original: **Nancy Levins**
 Present: **Nancy Levins,** heirs of
 Acreage: 400

Claimants:
 Original: **Joseph Hamelin, Junior**
 Present: **Joseph Hamelin, Junior**, heirs of
 Acreage: 400

To the class of improvement rights we have added, as above, the confirmation of the claim of the heirs of **Nancy Levins**, rejected before (document E) for want of sufficient ground.

We have also added, in the class of donations to the heads of families, the claim of **John Harbin** and **Henry Vanderburgh, Esq.**, in right of **Joseph Hamelin, Junior**, which we have confirmed to the heirs of the said Joseph Hamelin; John Harbin and Henry Vanderburgh having produced no evidence of transfer. This case had been before rejected (see document H, No.2).

(8:1:574)
Supplement to Document E

Stace McDonough, assignee of **Anthony Furney***.--The Board this day resumed the consideration of the claim of Stace McDonough, assignee, &c., rejected before for want of evidence, (see document E, accompanying their former report.) This claim was for four hundred acres, in right of improvement alleged to have been made by a certain **Anthony Forney***, on Patoka creek, in the winter of 1789 and 1790. [*so spelled] In support of the aforesaid claim, the deposition of **Solomon Thorn** taken before **Pierre Menard** and **George Fisher**, of Kaskaskias, in Randolph county, has been exhibited, (recorded book A page 327) stating that deponent, in the winter 1789 and 1790, saw at the slaty ford of Patoka creek, on the trace from Vincennes to Red Banks, an improvement, consisting of a cabin, wherein said Anthony Forney then lived, and a small field cleared of about half or three-quarters of an acre; and that deponent, in the summer following, saw the said field planted in corn, which was then in a flourishing condition. That Forney lived in Vincennes and neighborhood about eight or nine years, and then went away. It being known to one of the members of this Board, then in this country, that Anthony Forney was, in the year 1791, a boatman in the contractor's employ, and the danger from the Indians was at that period such that it is hardly probable that any man would venture to make a settlement twenty miles from Vincennes, (the real distance of the slaty ford) and could remain their unmolested. This circumstance gave rise to a strong suspicion of the truth of the statement made by said Solomon Thorn.

With a view to throw some light on the subject, the commissioners summoned Colonel **John Small**, who, being duly sworn, made the following deposition:

As to the improvement alluded to in the forementioned deposition, I have no knowledge of, neither do I think there was any such as stated by [**Solomon**] **Thorn** at that early date. My reasons for making this statement is, from the hostile disposition of the Indians at that period. AT that time said Thorn was an apprentice of mine; about which time I took occasion to send him, in company with others, to Patoka, on a hunting party; at which time they took an alarm of being about to be attacked by the Indians at their camp. The apprehension of danger was so great, that they decamped so precipitately as to leave a horse of mine near the camp, (this, I believe, was in the month of August,) which horse I never got till December following, at which time I went in company with Thorn in quest of him, into the neighborhood of Potoka. At which time I found the whole country, as far as I went, in a wild uncultivated state, not a vestige of improvement, neither do I recollect of every having heard of any in that quarter at that date. Thorn at that time was about from the age of fifteen to eighteen years, and those two forementioned trips all the opportunity he had of visiting that quarter about that time. As to Forney's residence at Vincennes, I have no knowledge of, further that I believe he had the superintendence of a boat for the contractor about that time, and frequented Vincennes occasionally. Thorn served me about the forementioned period five years; I, myself, have resided in this country every since the year 1785.

[signed] **John Small**

From the circumstances stated in the above deposition, and the result of the commissioners' inquiries of the ancient inhabitants of this place, who never knew of any such man residing here, further than is stated by John Small, and from the improbability of any man venturing so far from Vincennes, and remaining for such a space of time unmolested, the commissioners feel themselves under a strong impression that **Solomon Thorn**'s deposition is untrue, and cannot deem themselves justifiable in confirming the present claim; they do, therefore, reject it.

Stace McDonough, assignee of **Thomas Hill**.--A claim for four hundred acres in right of improvement stated to have been made by Thomas Hill at the Beech Bottom, (see document K). The deposition of the same **Solomon Thorn**, taken before the abovementioned **Pierre Menard** and **George Fisher**, states that said Thomas Hill, in the winter of 1789 and 1790, made an improvement and cultivation of Beech Bottom, one mile above **Anthony Forney's**, similar in every respect to said Forney's, and that Hill remained in the country till deponent's departure from Vincennes, which was about four years afterwards. Solomon Thorn's deposition in this case does not appear to be entitled to more credit than in the former. Except in Thomas Hill's not appearing to have been a boatman, every circumstance inducing suspicions in the former case obtrudes itself to the mind here, and the commissioners, under such an impression, cannot confirm this claim; they, therefore, reject it.

Richard Sinnet and **Patrick Carmichael.**--Each claim one hundred and thirty-six acres in right of improvement, opposite the old fort of Vincennes, rejected before for want of evidence, (see document F accomppanying their former report.)

The following depositions, taken before **Joseph Morgan** and **Jesse Hale, Esquires,** of Mercer county, Kentucky, appointef for that purpose by the commissioenrs, were exhibited, viz:

The deposition of **William Hall**, in support of the claim of **Patrick Carmichael** and **Richard Sinnet.**

The deposition of **Thomas Wilson**, in support of the same.

The deposition of **Richard Sinnet**, in support of the claim of **Patrick Carmichael.**

The first two depositions agree in stating that **Patrick Carmichael** and **Richard Sinnet** were soldiers under General -- **Clark**, went to Vincennes with him in the year 1779; that they applied to the Court for a grant of lands; that the same was granted to each of them to the amount, as **William Hall** says, of one hundred and sixty arpents, opposite the fort; that they cut timber thereon, and sawed planks for the use of the garrison, and made some brush heaps; that they could not raise corn there for the Indians. **William Hall** states that they were obliged to move over the river, within the French limits, to raise corn; and **Thomas Wilson**, that he understood they had raised corn elsewhere.

Richard Sinnet, in support of **Patrick Carmichael**'s claim, states nearly the same circumstances.

Thomas Wilson and **William Hall** left Vincennes in the summer of the year 1780.

Here appears neither improvement nor cultivation, nor does it appear that the claimants were ever residents in the country. The above claims are, therefore, rejected.

Robert Reynolds, assignee of **John** and **Matthew Garland, Moses** and **Adam Orth**.--Claims of four hundred acres, by virtue of improvements, in right of each of the several persons above mentioned. In support of these four claims were exhibited the depositions of **Solomon** and **Daniel Thorn**, stating the improvements and cultivation of **John** and **Matthew Garland, Adam** and **Moses Orth**, taken before **George Fisher**, of Kaskaskias, appointed by the commissioners to take depositions in the county of Randolph.

The said claims were rejected as founded on spurious testimony; by reference to the rejected cases (document E,) may be seen the reasons which induced the commissioners' decision.

They remain in the same opinion, still more convinced than ever that the deponent's statements are untrue. In justification of the perseverance in that opinion, they will observe, that the same **Daniel Thorn** who swore before the commissioners that the former depositions signed by his brother **Solomon [Thorn]** and himself were false, that he never knew either of the above original claimants, comes again as an evidence in the same case, and has made oath before **George Fisher** to establish the same facts he denied to have any knowledge of before.

They will observe, also, that none of the depositions taken before the said **George Fisher**, and exhibited to the commissioners, are signed by either **Solomon** or **Daniel Thorn**; they, therefore, reject them.

On the 17th of November, 1806, the Board went into the reconsideration of the claims of **James Gilbreath** for four hundred acres of land, by virtue of improvement, as assignee of **James Strong**. This claim had been rejected for want of sufficient evidence (see document E of rejected claims accompanying their former report.)

In support of the said claim were exhibited the depositions of **Solomon** and **Daniel Thorn**, taken before **George Fisher, Esquire**, of Kaskaskias, authorized by the commissioners for that purpose, stating the building of a cabin in the year 1787, fencing about one acre of ground, the planting and cultivating corn thereon for two years. The land is situate on Mehl's run, on waters of river Des Chis, and the residence of said **[James] Strong** in the country till the year 1792.

By reference to the document mentioned above, it will be seen, that, though the former and present depositions agree in stating improvements and cultivation, yet they differ materially respecting the continuance of **[James] Strong** in this country. The variation in the depositions of **Daniel Thorn** would be sufficient to invalidate his testimony; but **Solomon** and **Daniel Thorn**'s veracity appears very doubtful in the case of **James Reynolds** and **Stace McDonough**, rejected above; the commissioners viewing them both, but especially **Daniel [Thorn]**, as not entitled to credit, reject the present claims.

On the 18th day of November, [1806], took into consideration the claims of **Jean Baptiste L'Esperance** for a militia donation, which was rejected for want of evidence.

As the commissioners had established as a rule to admit as conclusive testimony no deposition filed and recorded in the Register's Office before their sittings began, except the deponent was dead, or such deposition operated against the claimant, and to have every witness examined before them, or, if at a distance, before persons by them appointed, they see themselves under the necessity of taking notice of this claim which had in their former report been improperly classed amongst those rejected for want of evidence.

Jean Baptiste L'Esperance had filed the deposition of **Pierre Bonneau** and **Louis Boyer**, stating that claimant had lived in Vincennes from the year 1782 to the year 1786, and performed militia duty during the said period.

This case does not come under the act of Congress of 1791; the claim is therefore rejected.

(ASP 8:1:575)

Supplement to No. 1 of Document H

With a view to invalidate the statement of the commissioners respecting the identity of the Cote a Beauchene and the Big Hill (Grande Cote) **Henry Vanderburgh, Esq.**, brought forward **Pierre Querre, alias Latulippe**, who, being sworn, made the following statement:

That he knew Mrs. -- **Cornoyer**'s father, his name was -- **Racine, called Beauchene**; he is not sure what his Christian name was, but he believed it to be Francois; that he knows that when the bans of matrimony were published between Mrs. -- **Cornoyer**, his only daughter, and her husband, **Pierre Cornoyer**, now deceased, she was therein called Angelique, the daughter of **Francois Racine**; that the hill now in or near the donation on the Fort Apparent old road, and about three miles eastward of Vincennes, has always been called the Big Hill; and that he, said

-- **Racine, dit Beauchene**, made a house there and cultivated some land thereon; that the deponent himself gathered melons therefrom

(ASP 8:1:576)

in **Racine**'s lifetime, who died in 1764 that he can now show the spot, or very near to it, that the hill called Beauchene's Cote is situate to the northeast of Vincennes, near the Wabash, about a league back of **Snapp's** mill; that Beauchene's Cote is a bigger hill than the one called the Big Hill; that the Big Hill and Cote a Beauchene bear nearly north and south, about a league apart from each other, and are entirely different spots; that the said -- **Racine dit Beauchene**, when he took up the Cote a Beauchene, rented the Grande Cote tract; that both were merely sugar camps, excepting the cultivation above mentioned; that he knew **Jean Baptiste Racine**, called **St. Marie**, who was late commandant at this plce; that he never was called Beauchene, but cousin-german of -- **Racine called Beauchene**.

Here it is to be observed, that the above deponent had said before, in the commissioners' office, that Grande Cote and Cote a Beauchene were the same hill, but requested not to be brought as an evidence for some prudential reasons which he then mentioned, but which are not now perfectly recollected.

That, notwithstanding the above deposition, the Cote a Beauchene and Big Hill (Grande Cote) are the same place, as the following extract from the orders of survey of **Winthrop Sargent**, then acting as Governor, book C, page 25, and the subjoined depositions, will fully demonstrate.

"**Robert Buntin** claims four hundred acres on the *Big Hill*, about three miles to the northeast of Vincennes, on the road leading to the Lick, by purchase from **Jacques Cardinal**. By the oath of **Esquire -- Edeline**, it is proved that **Jacques Cardinal** had permission to take up this land; and that, in 1782 and 1791, there were upon it twenty acres under good cultivation, to be satisfied by four hundred arpents."

Instead of a reference to our former report, (document H, No. 1) we insert here the order of survey granted to **Angelique Racine**, quoted therein and marked G.

"**Angelique Racine** four arpents by forty at the *Big Hill*, granted and allotted to her father **Francois Racine**, upward of thirty years ago, about three miles eastward of Vincennes."

It must be observed here, that the interference of the grant made to **Robert Buntin** at the *Big Hill* in right of **Jacques Cardinal**, with the one made at the same place to **Angelique Racine**, in right of her father, **Francois Racine**, and the last being partly included within the lines of the donation, prevented, as will be seen hereafter, the surveying of her claim, which to this day has remained unsurveyed.

Deposition of **John Small**

"I recollect having been called upon by Mrs. -- **Cornoyer**, I think four years since, as surveyor, to lay off a tract of land granted to the heirs of **Francois Racine** by the Governor. I accordingly went to the place appointed, which, as I have understood, has formerly been known by the name of Cote a Beauchene; Mr. **Pierre Querre, dit Latulippe**, being called upon, and then present, to point out and make known the improvement, in consequence of which the grant was made. I did not proceed to make the survey; the reasons why not are these: In the first place, the place pointed out by Latulippe, was within the lines of the old donation tract, No.24, then held and occupied by **Jeremiah Claypole**; and, secondly, **Robert Buntin, Esq.**, and **Joseph Baird** both protested against the surveys being made, insinuating that such a survey as was then and there required would eventually run through lands of theirs that were legally granted and regularly surveyed, and returned some time previous to that period. Upon which reasons I declined making the survey. The forementioned spot of land alluded to winthin lines near the Chemin Leglaize or Lick road, so called, about three and four miles from Vincennes, on the west side of Mill creek.

[Signed] **John Small**"

Robert Buntin's Deposition

"Some time in the year 1802, I was called upon by Mrs. -- **Cornoyer** to survey a tract of land of four arpents by forty, situate on the *Big Hill*, granted to **Angelique Racine**, in right of her father, **Francois Racine**. As this tract was said to interfere with a piece of land which I purchased from **Jacques Cardinal**, I declined acting as surveyor, and gave a copy of the order of survey to **John Small**, who had then been appointed surveyor by Governor -- **Harrison**, and accompanied him, together with the claimant, **Toussaint Dubois, Joseph Baird**, and **Pierre Querre, dit Latulippe**. Mr. Baird went with an intention of preventing the survey to be made, as he expected it would interfore with a tract of land claimed by him; and Querre went to show the precise spot where the improvement of the said **Francois Racine** was made. On our arrival at the place showed by Querre, (which is about three miles northeast of Vincennes,) it was found to be within the tract laid off and surveyed for donations to the heads of families at Vincennes; in consequence of which the survey was not made.

[signed] **Robert Buntin**"

Deposition of **Toussaint Dubois**

"I was with **Robert Buntin, John Small, Joseph Baird, Mrs. Cornoyer,** and **Pierre Querre, dit Latulippe,** at the time stated by Mr. Buntin, and saw the place pointed out by said Querre as the spot called for in the grant made to the father of Mrs. Cornoyer; it was on the *Grande Cote*, (Big Hill) called the *Cote a Beauchene.*

[signed] **Dubois**."

Thus it appears that Mrs. Cornoyer, formerly **Angelique Racine**, herself, and her witness **Pierre Querre, dit Latulippe**, when they went to show the place called for on the grant made to her, and the improvement made thereon, at the *Big Hill* (Grande Cote) showed indeed a *Big Hill*, but which was also called the *Cote a Beauchene.*

As to the deposition of **Pierre Querre**, (inserted above) the circumstances of his showing for the *Big Hill* the *Cote a Beauchene,* and now swearing that they are two distinct places, evinces the perversion of his morals, or derangement of his understanding, and effectually destroys the credibility of his testimony.

The commissioners deem it superfluous to make any further comment on this business, and adhere to the opinion expressed in their former report.

INDEX

Anderson, Thomas, 7
Anthis, Francis, 2
Anthis, Francis, 13
Arpin. See Francois Potdivin
Bailey, John, 2
Baird, Joseph, 30
Baird, Joseph, 30
Baird, Joseph, 31
Baird, Samuel, 2
Baird, Samuel, 11
Baird, Samuel, 20
Baird, Samuel, 22
Baker, Isaac, 2
Baker, Isaac, 13
Baker, Joel, 15
Barrackman, Abraham, 5
Barrackman, P., 14
Bazadone, Laurent, 22
Beauchene. See -- Racine
Beckes, B., 1
Beckes, B., 1
Beckes, B., 2
Becquet, --, widow of, 22
Berger, F., 2
Berger, F., 7
Berger, Frederick, 14
Biddle, E., 2
Biddle, E., 3
Biddle, F., 7
Biddle, Elias, 9
Biddle, Elias, 18
Black, James, 2
Black, Joseph, 7
Bolon, Hyppolite, 22
Bonneau, Pierre, 28
Bordeleau, Antoine, 15
Bordeleau, Antoine, heirs of, 15
Bosseron, Julie, 13
Bosseron, Ursule, 13
Boucher, Charles, 22
Boucher, Charles, heirs of, 22
Boucher, Vital, 15

Boyer, Louis, 28
Brossard, Joseph, 22
Brossard, Joseph, heirs or assigns of, 22
Brouillet, Francis, 16
Buntin, Robert, 5
Buntin, Robert, 9
Buntin, Robert, 9
Buntin, Robert, 11
Buntin, R., 12
Buntin, Robert, 12
Buntin, Robert, 14
Buntin, Robert, 17
Buntin, Robert, 17
Buntin, Robert, 29
Buntin, Robert, 30
Buntin, Robert, Esq., 30
Buntin, Robert, 30
Buntin, Robert, 31
Buntin, Robert, 31
Cantelmy, Francis, 22
Cardinal, --, 16
Cardinal, Marianne W., 22
Cardinal, --, widow, her heirs or assigns, 22
Cardinal, Jacques, 29
Cardinal, Jacques, 30
Cardinal, Jacques, 30
Carmichael, Patrick, 26
Carmichael, Patrick, 26
Carmichael, Patrick, 26
Carmichael, Patrick, 26
Carmichael, Patrick, 26
Carzee. See Garzee
Catt, George, 17
Catt, Philip, 2
Catt, P., 15
Clark, --, 26
Claypole, Jeremiah, 10
Claypole, Jeremiah, 16
Claypole, Jeremiah, 30
Clermont, Lizette, 22
Clermont, Lizette, heirs of, 22
Clermont, Michael, 23
Compagnotte, Francis, 16
Conger, Jonathan, 16
Conteaux, Jacques, 22
Conteaux, Jacques, heirs or assigns of, 22
Cornoyer, F., heirs of, 5
Cornoyer, --, Mrs., 28
Cornoyer, --, Mrs., 30

Cornoyer, --, Mrs., 30
Cornoyer, --, Mrs. 31
Cornoyer, --, Mrs. See Angelique Racine
Cornoyer, Pierre, 28
Crawford, John, 2
Crepeau, Louis, 22
Crepeau, Louis, heirs of, 22
Crock, D., 13
Crook, D., 2
Culbert, John, 20
Culbert, John, heirs of, 20
Dagenat, Ambroise, 23
Dagenat, Ambroise, heirs of, 23
Daly, John, 23
Danis, Honori, 16
Davis, John, 15
De Valcour, Francis M., 19
Decker, A., 2
Decker, Isaac, heirs of, 14
Decker, Joseph, 2
Decker, Joseph, 13
Decker, J., 6
Decker, Luke, Esq., 6
Decker, M., 3
Decker, Tobias, 6
Decker, T., 6
Decoteau. See Joseph Lecoteau
Delaurier, Jean Baptiste, 16
Delaurier, Jean Baptiste, 18
Delaurier, Jean Baptiste, & wife, 20
Dempsey, Hugh, 20
Desloges. See Pierre Poirier
Ditard. See Jean St. Louis
Dobbins, Matthew, 20
Dobbins, Matthew, heirs of, 20
Dubois, Toussaint, 3
Dubois, Toussaint, 4
Dubois, Toussaint, 4
Dubois, Toussaint, 10
Dubois, Toussaint, 14
Dubois, Jean Baptiste, 17
Dubois, Toussaint, 30
Dubois, Toussaint, 31
Duchesne, Jean Baptiste, 16
Dumay, --, 16
Dumay, --, heirs of, 16
Durham, John, 3
Edeline, --, Esq., 29
Edger, John, 15

Egbert, Nicholas, 9
Falls, R., 8
Fields, Keen, 4
Fisher, George, 24
Fisher, George, 25
Fisher, George, 27
Fisher, George, 27
Fisher, George, 27
Fisher, George, Esq., 27
Foizy, Francois, 20
Foreman, Joseph, 7
Foreman, Joseph, 11
Forney, Anthony, 24
Forney, Anthony, 25
Furney, Anthony, 24
Gamelin, Antoine, 17
Gamelin, Antoine, widow & heirs of, 17
Garland, John, 27
Garland, Matthew, 27
Garzee, Jean, 1
Gibson, John, 3
Gibson, John, 4
Gilbreath, James, 27
Glaze, Adam, 17
Goder, Pierre, 23
Goder, Rene, 21
Goyeau, Antoine, 1
Gracet. See Gracoit
Gracoit, John, 1
Grimarre, Jean Baptiste, 1
Grimarre, Pierre, Senior, 23
Grimarre, Pierre, Senior, heirs of, 23
Guiyeau, Pierre, heirs of, 1
Hale, Jesse, Esq., 26
Hall, William, 26
Hall, William, 26
Hall, William, 26
Hamelin, Francois, 2
Hamelin, Joseph, Junior, 24
Hamelin, Joseph, Junior, heirs of, 24
Hamelin, Joseph, Junior, 24
Harbin, John, 1
Harbin, John, 10
Harbin, John, 13
Harbin, John, 24
Harbin, Joshua, 1
Harbin, Joshua, heirs of, 1
Harbin, Joshua, heirs of, 4
Harbin, Joshua, heirs of, 14

Harness, Adam, 6
Harpier, Jean Baptiste, 17
Harpin, Amable, 2
Harrison, William H., 16
Harrison, William H., 16
Harrison, --, Governor, 30
Heinemann. See Hyneman
Hill, Thomas, 25
Holder, Thomas, 5
Holliday, Ezekiel, 2
Howell, John, 17
Howell, John, heirs & assignees of, 17
Hunot, Antoine, heirs of, 2
Hunot, Gabriel, 2
Hunot, Joseph, Junior, 2
Hyneman, Robert, 10
James Johnson, 1
Johnson, James, Esq., 1
Johnson, James, 1
Johnson, James, turner, 2
Johnson, James, 2
Johnson, James, Esq., 2
Johnson, James, 4
Johnson, James, Esq., 8
Johnson, James, 13
Johnson, James, Esq., 19
Johnson, John, 3
Johnson, John, 13
Johnson, John, Junior, 3
Johnson, Richard, 3
Johnson, William, 11
Johnston, Robert, 3
Jones, John R., 3
Jones, J. R., 13
Jones, Thomas, 3
Jordon, Ephraim, 21
Jordon, Thomas, 3
Jordon, Thomas, 9
Joyeuse, Joseph, 3
L'Esperance, Jean Baptiste, 28
L'Esperance, Jean Baptiste, 28
Lachine, --, 16
Laderoute, Jacques, 6
Lafeuillade, Jean Baptiste, 6
Lafferty, John, 6
Lafleur, Joseph, dit Perodo, 5
Lafontaine, Etienne, 5
Laforest, Louis, 6
Laforest, Pierre, 4

Laforest, Pierre, 18
Lalumier, Antoine, dit Petit, 6
Lamotte, Joseph, 5
Langlois, Francois, 4
Languedoc, Andre, 18
Languedoc, Andre, 18
Languedoc, Francis, 17
Laplante, Jean Baptiste, 19
Lapointe, Joseph, dit Orleans, 3
Lardoise, Amable, Junior, 5
Latour, Pierre, 3
Latulippe. See Pierre Querre
Lecoteau, Joseph, 5
Ledgerwood, James 5
Ledgerwood, James, 10
Ledgerwood, James, 14
Ledgerwood, --, 15
Lee, William, 5
Lefeuillade, Francois, 4
Lefeuillade, Pierre, 4
Lefevre, Antoine, 3
Lefevre, Louis, 6
Lefleur, --, 18
Legarde, Jean, 5
Legrand, Jean M., 4
Legrand, Jean Baptiste, 5
Legrand, Joseph, 4
Leproux, Joseph, 18
Letemps, Jean Baptiste, 4
Levins, Nancy, 23
Levins, Nancy, heirs of, 23
Levins, Nancy, heirs of, 24
Levins, Nicholas, 18
Levron, Louis, dit Meteye, 17
Levron, Louis, heirs of, 17
Lindey, Frederick, 4
Lindey, Frederick, 18
Lismain, Peter, 1
Loneveu, Louis, 5
Lowe, John, 6
Lubuxierre, Louis, 4
Maisonville, Jean Baptiste, 8
Maisonville, Joseph, Junior, 8
Mallett, F., heirs of, 20
Marie, Antoine, 19
Marie, Antoine, heirs of, 19
Marshall, John, 18
Martin, John, 1
Martin, John, 1

Martin, John, 7
Martin, Alexander, 7
Martin, Alexander, heirs of, 7
Martin, Alexander, 7
Martin, Jean Baptiste, 8
Matson, Ralph, 7
Mayes, Jeremiah, 7
Mayes, Robert, 7
Mayes, W., 3
Mayes, William, 7
Mayes, W., 13
Mays, Robert, 21
Mays, Robert, heirs of, 21
McClure, Samuel, 4
McDonough, Stace, 24
McDonough, Stace, 25
McDonough, Stace, 28
McGowen, William, 7
McIntosh, William, 4
McIntosh, William, 8
McIntosh, William, 10
McIntosh, William, 12
Mehl, Frederick, 13
Melloche, Antoine, 8
Menard, Pierre, 6
Menard, Pierre, 24
Menard, Pierre, 25
Meredy, Daniel, 8
Meteye. See Louis Levron
Mette, Joseph, 8
Mette, Rene, 7
Midler, Frederick, 8
Mills, John, heirs of, 1
Mills, John, heirs of, 3
Mills, J., heirs of, 8
Mills, John, heirs of, 12
Mills, John, heirs of, 12
Mills, Zachariah, 4
Mills, Zachariah, 5
Monviel, Joseph, 8
Moore, Samuel, 21
Morgan, Joseph, Esq., 26
Morin De Valcour, Francis, 19
Morin, Francis, dit De Valcour, 23
Morrison, William, heirs of, 6
Morrison, William, heirs of, 9
Moyse, Charles, 7
Mulliken, James, 18
Mulliken, James, heirs of, 18

Murphey, John, 7
Orleans. See Joseph Lapointe
Orth, Adam, 27
Orth, Moses, 27
Ouellette, Alexis, 8
Pacquin, Francis, 21
Page, Joseph, 9
Pea, A., 3
Pea, Abraham, 21
Pea, Daniel, 5
Pea, Daniel, 9
Pea, D., 9
Pea, Henry, 1
Pea, Henry, 8
Pea, Henry, 10
Pea, John, 9
Pea, J., 9
Pea, Jacob, 9
Pea, J., 15
Pea, Jacob, Junior, 19
Pea, John, heirs of, 9
Perodo. See Joseph Lafleur
Perron, Pierre, Junior, 23
Perron, Pierre, heirs of, 23
Peters, Godfrey, 9
Petit. See Antoine Lalumier
Pettier, Andrew, 23
Pettier, Andrew, heirs of, 23
Pettier, Marie J., 19
Poirier, Francois, 9
Poirier, Pierre, dit Desloges, 10
Potdivin, Francois, dit Arpin, 9
Potdivin, Jean Baptiste, 9
Potdivin, Joseph, 9
Preville, Louis, 10
Purcell, John, 11
Querre, Pierre, Junior, 10
Querre, Pierre, & wife, 19
Querre, Pierre, alias Latulippe, 28
Querre, Pierre, dit Latulippe, 30
Querre, Pierre, dit Latulippe, 30
Querre, Pierre, dit Latulippe, 31
Querre, Pierre, dit Latulippe, 31
Racine, Andrew, dit St. Marie, 19
Racine, Angelique, 28
Racine, Angelique, 29
Racine, Angelique, 30
Racine, Angelique, 31
Racine, Francois, 28

Racine, Francois, 29
Racine, Francois, 30
Racine, Francois, 31
Racine, --, dit Beauchene, 28
Racine, --, dit Beauchene, 29
Racine, Jean Baptiste, 20
Racine, Jean Baptiste, heirs of, 20
Racine, Jean Baptiste, dit St. Marie, 29
Ramsay, A., 2
Ramsay, A., 6
Ramsay, Allen, 11
Ramsay, A., 13
Raux, --, 19
Ravalet, Louis, 19
Reed, Benjamin, heirs of, 18
Reed, John, 11
Reed, Walker, 1
Reed, William, 9
Reed, William, 18
Reel, John, 7
Reynolds, James, 28
Reynolds, Robert, assignee, 27
Riend, Joseph, 10
Rimbault, Henry, 10
Robbins, John, 10
Robbins, John, heirs of, 10
Robert, Pierre, 10
Roderigue, Diego, 11
Ruyard, Joseph, 10
Saint Aubin. See St. Aubin
Saint Louis. See St. Louis
Saint Marie. See St. Marie
Sampson, Alexander, 21
Sargent, Winthrop, 29
Savage, John, 21
Savage, John, heirs of, 21
Sentier, Olivier, 20
Severe, Louis, 12
Shoebrooks, Edward, 12
Simarre, Francois, 12
Simpson, P., 5
Simpson, Patrick, 12
Sinnet, Richard, 26
Sinnet, Richard, 26
Sinnet, Richard, 26
Sinnet, Richard, 26
Sinnet, Richard, 26
Small, John, 4
Small, John, 17

Small, John, 21
Small, John, 25
Small, John, 25
Small, John, 30
Small, John, 30
Small, John, 30
Small, John, 31
Small, Thomas, 11
Small, Thomas, 15
Smith, Anthony, 12
Smith, Anthony, 12
Smith, Daniel, 7
Smith, Daniel, 11
Smith, Daniel, 13
Smith, William, 11
Smith, William, heirs of, 11
Smith, William T., 11
Snapp, Abraham T., 5
Snapp, Abraham, 10
Snapp, Abraham F., 11
Snapp, Abraham F., 11
Snapp, Abraham F., 21
Snapp, --, 29
Soulier, Jean Louis, 12
Spears, Noah, 3
St. Louis, Jean, dit Ditard, 11
St. Aubin, Louis, 11
St. Marie, Andre, 12
St. Marie. See Andrew Racine
St. Marie. See Jean Baptiste Racine
Stokely, Francis, 12
Store, Frederick, 12
Strong, James, 27
Strong, James, 27
Strong, James, 27
Sullivan, Daniel, heirs of, 18
Tessier, Francois, 14
Tevebaugh, Jacob, 10
Theil, Isaac, 13
Thiriot, Jean C., widow of, 23
Thiriot, Julie, 23
Thomas, J., 7
Thorn, Charles, 13
Thorn, Daniel, 13
Thorn, Daniel, 27
Thorn, Daniel, 27
Thorn, Daniel, 27
Thorn, Daniel, 27
Thorn, Daniel, 28

Thorn, Daniel, 28
Thorn, Jacob, 13
Thorn, Michael, 13
Thorn, Michael, 14
Thorn, Michael, 14
Thorn, Michael, Junior, 13
Thorn, Peter, 13
Thorn, Solomon, 14
Thorn, Solomon, 25
Thorn, Solomon, 25
Thorn, Solomon, 25
Thorn, Solomon, 27
Thorn, Solomon, 27
Thorn, Solomon, 27
Thorn, Solomon, 27
Thorn, Solomon, 28
Tougas, Auguste, 13
Tougas, Jean Baptiste, 20
Tougas, Jean Baptiste, heirs of, 20
Tougas, Joseph, Junior, 14
Tougas, William, 14
Valcour, Jean Baptiste, 14
Valcour, De. See De Valcour
Vanderburgh, Henry, 1
Vanderburgh, Henry, 2
Vanderburgh, Henry, 3
Vanderburgh, Henry, 4
Vanderburgh, Henry, 5
Vanderburgh, Henry, 8
Vanderburgh, Henry, 9
Vanderburgh, Henry, 12
Vanderburgh, Henry, 14
Vanderburgh, Henry, 14
Vanderburgh, Henry, Esq., 24
Vanderburgh, Henry, Esq., 28
Vigo, Francis, 5
Vigo, F., 12
Villeneuve, Charles, 14
Watson, William, 7
Watts, James, 21
Watts, James, heirs of, 21
Wells, William, 5
Wells, William, 9
Wells, William, 14
Westfall, Abraham, 14
Westfall, John N., 14
Williams, F., 2
Wilmore, John, 15
Wilson, Isaac, 15

Wilson, A., heirs of, 15
Wilson, Thomas, 26
Wilson, Thomas, 26
Wilson, Thomas, 26
Wyant, Christopher, 15

www.ingramcontent.com/pod-product-compliance
Lightning Source LLC
Chambersburg PA
CBHW080410300426
44113CB00015B/2469